I0467835

The
TIGHTROPE
of
MIDDLE
MANAGEMENT

MAINTAINING YOUR BALANCE

Jack T Baker

ISBN: 1500602140
ISBN 13:9781500602147
Library of Congress Control Number: 2014913280
CreateSpace Independent Publishing Platform
North Charleston, South Carolina

TABLE OF CONTENTS

PREFACE

There probably aren't many of you who remember the TV show "This Is Your Life," but the following could have been an episode about the life of a middle manager. An episode that explored the perceptions and the realities of a person who has been a member of the "system" for more than forty years. A system that rewards teamwork, demands loyalty, expects its leaders to get the job done, defines reality in a way that supports its objectives, and expects its members to embrace the policies and procedures that have been developed to keep all the parts greased and the wheels on the track. Unfortunately, it is also a system that frustrates you and forces you to question your very being.

There are many who will tell you how to manage, lead, influence, improve, or control the people who do the "work." They will say it is your responsibility to make the system perform and there is no shortage of experts who claim they have the solutions to your problems and your shortcomings. But then, regardless of the issue at hand, if something doesn't work it is your responsibility to fix it.

I can no longer buy what they are selling. I've begun to rail against what I've been taught and what I have taught. Some will argue I'm too negative, some will suggest I "just don't get it," others will suggest I just don't have what it takes. I will accept that I am tired, that I am getting close to being burned out, but I believe the world I will describe, the world that I live in, is more realistic and more relevant than the one described by the consultants and the experts. I believe the how-to books make it sound easier than it is. I believe the secret to being a successful middle manager depends upon your ability to walk a very fine line. There are few concrete answers, there are few right ways, and there are precious few answers. Maintaining balance is the key.

This book is dedicated to all those who are in the trenches, to those who make it work, to those who are not afraid to get their hands dirty, and to those who are constantly dealing with the wants and needs of the people who work for them, the people they work for, and all the people who influence the process. Hopefully, what I have come to learn late in the process will be of benefit to all those who have, are, or will be facing the same issues. The answers are not in the textbooks; they are not in the consultant's Power Point presentation. The answers are with the ones who are living the experience. My story is no better, or worse, or different than yours. We all deal with the same issues, we all are expected to "make it happen."

While it is my hope that describing my journey will help others make more informed decisions, I'll be happy if someone just says: "Your experiences are my experiences; your questions are my questions; your perspective has informed mine; we are in the same place. We are on the same tightrope and you have helped me gain or maintain my balance."

INTRODUCTION
THE WORLD OF MIDDLE MANAGEMENT

This book describes the life of middle managers, that group of people who are caught in the middle, the ones who make it all work but get beat up every day. From my vantage point they are in a no-win situation. There are customers, consultants, academics, and bosses who will tell us to manage better, to get more done, to solve the problem, to lead the work force, and to create win-win encounters. Can anyone really do all those things? Is there a textbook out there that has all the answers? Is there a management or leadership theory that will guarantee success? But then what is the definition of success? What does it take to be a successful middle manager? We are on a tightrope. How do you keep from falling off, let alone moving forward?

There are thousands of how-to books out there. There are many who give seminars on leading, on strategic planning, on goal setting, and on how to "deal with people," but from my perspective, there aren't any books that tell it like it is. What do you do when an employee tells you "I don't care what you say; you are not going to change what I believe"? What do you do when an employee says his supervisor was mean to him? What do you say to your boss when he says, "Just get it done" but then criticizes you for the decision that was made. Or worse yet, when something goes wrong, says, "I never told you to do that." Please don't repeat the management/leadership speech. I know it's not my job to control beliefs, just behavior. I know we need to make sure we treat all employees with respect – but define "mean." And please not the "how to deal with your boss" speech. Saying it and doing it are two different things.

Translating the vision to action is much more difficult, much more complex, than the how-to books suggest or the management consultants would like you to believe. The truths that we face every day, the polarities that we have to balance, include some very complex issues. For example:

- People want a black or white world and yes or no decisions; but, in reality, there is seldom anything but gray.

- People want work (life) to be equal and fair but work (life) is neither.

- To further complicate the middle manager's life there are many conflicting concepts, philosophies, and theories that must be dealt with:

  - efficiency vs. effectiveness,

  - leadership vs. management,

  - strategic planning vs. tactical action,

  - perception vs. reality (whatever that is).

As middle managers navigate through the conflicting goals, objectives, policies, practices, and directives, they are reacting to contradictions on three levels. On the surface, they are trying to get the job done, they are trying to herd all the cats and go in one direction. Below the surface, they are seeking the right (or perhaps most appropriate) management and/or leadership theory to help them interact with those they work for, those who work for them, and all those who influence the process. Finally, there is a deeper internal struggle as one asks, "Why am I putting up with all this grief?...it sure is not the money."

In the following pages, I explore these levels of "existence." I look at the life and times of middle managers and I view the tightrope we are on from the customer's perspective, the worker's perspective, and from our boss's vantage point. Hopefully, this view of the realities of middle management will help all of us understand the forces that are at play, because in order to be successful you need to walk the walk, not just talk the talk. To be successful, you need to see the big picture but stay focused on the weeds. To be successful, you'd better be able to lead by example, not by some theory. To be successful, you need to stay on the tightrope.

I admit I see the world of middle management from a narrow, unique point of view. I'm not suggesting it is any better, or any worse, than anyone else's, it is simply the window I have.

I'm a facility engineer, a middle manager, and I, like many others, live on that tightrope. I am expected to think strategically, yet it seems as if I am always reacting to the latest panic, the latest customer complaint. Most days my planning horizon is today, not tomorrow, certainly not five years from now. But then I wonder, is that reactive mode a self-fulfilling prophecy – if I am constantly reacting will I ever have time to solve the problem that is causing today's panic?

I know there are many who live in this world. Michael Kingley, in an essay in Time Magazine (July 6, 1988), describes his foray into middle management after years of "flying solo" and noted it took some getting used to. He sought answers to the inevitable question of how do you lead, manage, or both, and states that the books and the articles telling him how often contradict themselves, let alone each other. He concludes that as a middle manager, he often finds himself asking the classic question: "Why listen to experts? What do they know?" I share his frustration because I've been asking the same questions for nearly 40 years.

I acknowledge I am happiest when I am "in the trenches" working with those who swing the hammers or run the power plants, but I have also been at the other end of the spectrum. I have been a policy maker, a consultant, an instructor. I know the theory. I have written the policies. I have taught others how it should be done. But I was unhappy in those roles. It is easy to expect clear-cut decisions to be made when you don't have to make them. It is easy to be an inspector and tell people what they should be doing. However, I knew that when I was in the "real world" I couldn't do what I was preaching. I believe management, let alone leadership, is a performing art, not a science.

I also believe an understanding of this middle ground is important – important for those who lead us, because they think strategically and get frustrated with us; for those we lead, because they also get frustrated with us and wonder why we can't fix things; and for us, the ones in the middle, because we have to walk the tightrope and get frustrated with both sides. We all face the same problems; we all deal with the situations I will describe. Your examples, your frustrations, are as real as mine. We are in the same boat. Over the years I've grown tired of conferences and workshops because the answers are not there, but those events do provide two very important reminders. First, you find your situation is no different than anyone else's. It is good to be reminded that you are not the only one dealing with these issues. Second, it is always important to remind yourself that your organization is not as bad as you think.

Hopefully, this book will provide those insights as well and describe what really happens so everyone can better understand the one caught in the middle. Perhaps with this knowledge, we can avoid following the well-beaten path of others. The 1990s were, and the new century is, characterized as a period of constant white water, a period of constant change, a period when hard decisions have to be made if we are to "manage" in this complex, information rich world. The public sector, as well as the private sector, is restructuring and downsizing in order to remain competitive in the world environment and both sectors are questioning practices, policies, and procedures that govern the way they "do business." This constant state of turmoil forces all of us to take a second look at how we do our jobs. If we don't understand how each side views the changes, the dynamics that affect the processes, or the ramification of the decision to challenge organizational cultures, I believe we are destined for hard times and most likely failure in our efforts to improve. A better understanding of our world, the processes that allocate limited resources, and the perspective of the ones doing the work, is the very foundation of leadership, whether it be in the arena of facility maintenance or automobile manufacturing. "Leadership has to step outside the culture that created the leader and start evolutionary change processes that are more adaptive. This ability to understand the limitations of one's culture and to develop and adaptive culture is the essence and ultimate challenge of leadership" (Schein, 1992).

As you explore the culture of your organization, you have to appreciate that there are many players influencing your path. As we work to meet the needs of the customers, we are often accused of not taking care of those who work for us. The employees who have challenged me, who have sought me out, don't trust "management." They don't believe they are being treated fairly. They suggest that our efforts to provide more flexible service to the customer, our efforts to reorganize, and efforts to be more productive are threats to their livelihood. Over the years some of them have used a variety of forums to lash out at the perceived inequities. What are their complaints? Some theories suggest that if we include them in the process they will support the path we must take. Will they agree? Can we come together?

Equally as important, their supervisors deserve to be heard. Some, who have worked in this business for years, don't agree with my objectives. They see the future as nothing but turmoil. They have seen new approaches come and go over the years and suggest that all of this change simply must be "lived through." Are they right? Can I understand their perspective; can they see mine? Finally, there are the bosses, the leadership, and the administrators, the "system." Over the years I've worked for a variety of people, each with their own management and leadership style. What do they expect from me; how do they see this world? What perspective do they share? These are questions that need to be asked and perhaps the answer can be found on a hand-painted signboard that my wife and I discovered on a weekend drive, a drive designed to get away from the stress, the conflicts of my job. The author may say it all when he or she asks:

WHAT IF WHAT YOU BELIEVE CREATES YOUR REALITY?

CHAPTER I
MIDDLE MANAGEMENT: WHY WOULD ANYONE WANT THIS JOB?

I have asked myself many times over the years what came first – did I get into this profession because of my make-up, my personality, or has my make-up, my personality, been the reason my profession has consumed me, frustrated me, and raised so many questions? I'm an admitted workaholic; 12 hour days have been the norm from the beginning. The Myers-Briggs personality type indicator (Keirsey & Bates, 1984) codes me as an ESTJ (extrovert, sensing, thinking, judging). I am impatient; I trust facts; I like logical order; and I want decisions made. The Johari window behavioral style (Marston, 1928) suggests that I'm political and want freedom from control and detail—that I'm logical but calculating, that I can be seen as overly confident, unrealistic, and even glib. I see myself as one who others come to in order to get the job done and I make little time for those who find reasons why it can't be done. But over time I have become very critical of those who suggest that new or different management procedures, models, and techniques can solve workplace problems.

What does it take to be a facility engineer (a middle manager)? It has to be more than an occupation, a job; and the job must be more than pouring concrete and constructing buildings (or fill in the blank). There must be more than applying formulas; there must be more than finding methods to increase productivity and answering customer complaints. There must be a way to understand the complexities and the tensions that shape the way people sharing our world act, react, and exist.

Boyle's Law.

"If not controlled, work will flow to the competent man until he submerges"

-Charles Boyle of NASA

The middle manager is often tasked with creating a world that provides a straightforward approach to the allocation of resources (funding and staffing) yet we live in a world that deals with the realities of political decisions, inefficiencies, and conflicting priorities and objectives. What does it take to keep a foot in each of these worlds? What motivates one to walk the tightrope, to stay on a path that provides little opportunity to control one's own destiny? We have little ability to garner the resources needed to provide the services required by the customer and that reality results in seemingly constant criticism by those who believe their needs are not given the proper priority. What is it like to try to balance the conflicting objectives? What must one do to stay the course?

Stepping On The Tight Rope

Little did I know, or understand, that as I was stepping around, over, and sometimes on the protesters blocking the door of the

Engineering building, that those steps were, in fact, my first steps off the platform onto my tightrope. It was 1969; college campuses were in crisis; students wanted the United States out of Vietnam; the place was going crazy, and I wanted in that building. What were these people doing? I had to finish my research. Who was paying their bills? I had responsibilities; I had to move on. As I reflect on those days I now realize they were the first small steps that would set my path for most, if not all, of my adult life. Over the years there haven't been many detours. I've worked hard to stay on the path but I now find I'm the one protesting. I've worked for the "system" in a number of capacities, literally around the world, and I've supported it; I've believed in it; I've accepted it as the way it had to be. I've taken all the management courses; I've even taught them. I know how it is supposed to work, but I have also seen how it really works during budget hearings on Capitol Hill. I've also seen reality on a flight line at 2 a.m. when a young airman, who had never seen snow before, was trying to replace a bolt on a 20-ton snow plow. With his hands turning blue he climbed back into the cab, fell in line with four other trucks and started down the runway. Traveling 40 miles an hour with only blinking lights to guide him, he had 15 minutes to clear the runway before the plane arrived. How do you motivate a young man in this situation? What would the management books say to this 18-year- old, away from home for the first time in his life, with the lives of others literally at his freezing fingertips?

My eyes catch the poem I have hanging on my wall, "The Calf's Path", by Samuel Walter Foss (1858-1911). I first saw the poem in 1972 while attending an Air Force school that was teaching me how to be an engineering officer. Maybe it was a premonition of things to come, but the poem really made an impression. I was going to copy it, but didn't. Two years later I was in Southeast Asia, and saw it again as I was trying to figure out why I was there. I had learned a lot in two years; I had seen many examples of what the poem was teaching. I found a local craftsman who made it into a plaque and I've had it with me ever since.

The Calf's Path

One day, through the primeval wood,
A calf walked home, as good calves should;
But made a trail all bent askew,
A crooked trail as all calves do.
Since then two hundred years have fled,
And, I infer, -- the calf is dead.
But still he left behind this trail,
And thereby hangs my moral tale.
. . . continues . . .

How could I have known that my chosen profession (engineering) and my first job (an alternative to the draft), would become my life, my calling, in many ways my being, yet a constant source of tension? How do I reconcile a need to support, to be committed to, to believe in what the "system" expects while at the same time disagreeing with it, resenting it, and at times ignoring it because it doesn't let me get the things done that I know need to be completed?

The trail was taken up next day
By a lone dog that passed that way;
And then a wise bell-wether sheep
Pursued the trail o'er vale and steep,
And drew the flock behind him, too,
As good bell-wethers always do.
And from that day, o'er hill and glade,
Through those old woods a path was made;
And many men wound in and out,
And dodged, and turned, and bent about
And uttered words of righteous wrath
Because t'was such a crooked path.
But still they followed -- do not laugh --
The first migrations of the calf,
And through this winding wood-way stalked
Because he wobbled when he walked.
. . . continues . . .

For over 40 years I have walked my path. My education, my professional background, my very being (and that of many of the people who work in this business) expect things to be black or white, to have solutions that are concrete, rock solid and "correct" from a cost/benefit point of view. Meanwhile, those I worked for in the past and currently work for, live in another world. They expect the lights to come on; they expect the room to be cool in summer, warm in winter. They are dealing with "bigger" issues: business decisions, academic programs; they believe the facilities are there to serve them and rightfully so. They expect them to work and expect me to make it happen! Unfortunately, the reality of the world this relationship exists in, the environment in which these players interact, is neither as black or white, nor as pure as the engineers and technicians would like, nor as clear-cut or as simple as the customer supposes. But since this is only a "job," since it's only a way to make a living, why do I take it so personally? Why does the following cut me to the bone?

DORM RESIDENTS LOSE HEATING
(CAMPUS NEWSPAPER)

With temperatures estimated in the 20s dropping into the single digits, and with a wind chill advisory in effect, a broken heating line shut down the heating system for dorm residents yesterday from about 3 a.m. to 4 p.m. (Sunday). A pipe services employee with the Physical Plant, who did not want to be identified, said the problem was caused by a rusted heating line that broke, and it took about eight hours for the department to fix. He said fixing a heating problem like yesterday's usually takes about eight hours because "you need to drain all the water out of the heating system." "In a building with nine floors and a heating unit in each individual room, that's going to take some time," the employee added.

The article goes on and quotes a student: . . . "THEY SHOULD HAVE PEOPLE READY AND WAITING TO FIX THINGS LIKE THIS," a student complained. "OUR PARENTS PAY ENOUGH MONEY FOR US TO COME HERE THAT WE SHOULD HAVE HEAT."

Yes, I agree; they do pay good money; they should expect the facilities to work, but we can't afford to have people standing by waiting for something to break. It's not that easy; don't they understand? Meanwhile, a member of the faculty provides his perspective: "I have just returned from teaching a class of 180 students and am saturated with perspiration even though the outdoor temperature is only in the 20's. I am sure my students were just as uncomfortable as I was. It requires little imagination to deduce that the problem is caused by the large amount of body heat generated by the continuous stream of large classes held in this room and that this room (in fact, the entire building) requires year-round climate control, i.e. air-conditioning, to remove the heat gain. The problem of excessive heat in this building is no different today that it was ten years ago when I last taught in this building despite the advances in HVAC equipment and control in the interim.

I urge you to take an active role is solving the problem of maintaining climate control in all of the classrooms throughout the university. The problem cannot be solved by telephone calls to the service desk -- I have tried this approach many times and have not received a satisfactory response.

The solution to the problem requires policy decisions and direction from your office. I strongly believe that your department has an obligation to both students and faculty to provide them with an atmosphere within which they can perform at their best." (Excerpt from a letter sent to the Director of Physical Plant).

Wait a minute; tell it like it is, the budget -- the aging infrastructure -- the decaying campus -- requirements are outstripping our resources. Tell them it sounds easy but it is not. But they don't care; they expect things to work. Who can blame them? The customer is always right; we should provide them the facilities they need to do their job. We're trying, but which number one priority is in fact number one?

On one hand you have a world that wants, demands structure -- a world that needs a rational approach to decision making.

On the other hand, you have a world that must deal with the political realities of the public sector. In this world, efficiency often falls prey to effectiveness. Unfortunately, effectiveness has to compete with trying to maintain a balance between competing priorities. The Calf's Path continues:

> This forest path became a lane,
> That bent, and turned, and turned again;
> This crooked lane became a road,
> Where many poor horse with his load
> Toiled on beneath the burning sun,
> And traveled some three miles in one.
> And thus a century and a half
> They trod the footsteps of the calf.
> The years passed on in swiftness fleet,
> The road became a village street;
> And this, before men were aware,
> A city's crowded thoroughfare;
> And soon the central street was this
> Of a renowned metropolis;
> And men two centuries and a half
> Trod in the footsteps of that calf.
> Each day a hundred thousand rout
> Followed the zigzag calf about;
> And o'er his crooked journey went
> The traffic of a continent.
> A hundred thousand men were led
> By one calf near three centuries dead.
> They followed still his crooked way;
> And lost one hundred years a day;
> For thus such reverence is lent
> To well-established precedent.
> . . . continues . . .

Maybe, just maybe, it's the nature of the beast -- it's the walk I've chosen. I'm good at it but there has to be more, continuing:

A moral lesson this might teach,
Were I ordained and called to preach;
For men are prone to go it blind
Along the calf-paths of the mind,
And work away from sun to sun
To do what other men have done.
They follow in the beaten track
And out and in, and forth and back,
And still their devious course pursue
To keep, the path that others do.
But how the wise old wood-gods laugh,
Who saw the first primeval calf!
Ah! many things this tale might teach
But I am not ordained to preach.

The Trip Begins

The day started out like any other and promised to be yet another day on the tightrope. After gulping down a second cup of coffee I began to read the e-mail, a management craze (it was that in 1994, it is so much more today) that was supposed to make our jobs easier; after all, we now have more information at our fingertips. Since I was still having trouble changing my management practices after so many years, I reviewed paper copies of what was on the screen. Five of the seven sheets (today there are hundreds) went into the recycle box, today's trashcan. The other two? Both customer complaints. The first suggested our painters were slow and "weird." Weird, what does that mean? I get nothing but praise for our painters; they are my best ambassadors. I had the urge to toss this one in the box but

I wanted to find out if the customer was "weird." The second? It contained the complaints of a customer who said it had been days since the heat worked and no one had shown up. That appeared to be a "real" problem. The customer went on to say: "Does anyone know what is happening? Don't you know what the equipment does? We keep getting the runaround." My first thought was to jump on the information highway and down the customer's throat. I'm five people short in this work center. I can't hire qualified people; the salaries are a joke. Yes, we know what we are doing. But wait, that is not a very customer-oriented response; that is not going to solve anything; besides I have a nagging feeling we probably did give them the runaround. Why did it take so long to respond? Before I hit the send button, I look to my office wall. My wife's needlepoint stares back at me: "Lord help me to be patient and I mean now!" I turn to the other wall and my customer poster stares back: "If we don't take care of the customer, someone else will."

What do I do now? What does the customer expect? Do they want an explanation? I doubt it; they just want the heat to work. How do I prevent a reoccurrence? Why did it happen in the first place? The management books would suggest a review of the process; they would recommend pushing authority down to the lowest level; they would imply that the "system" was at fault not the employee. On one hand I believe that, yet on the other I'm afraid someone simply didn't do his/her job. I'm convinced if I ask the supervisor what happened his answer would be the same as my initial response. I run the conversation through my mind; I know the words by heart; it's repeated every day. There has to be a better way, or is there? My head aches already; it's off to the next conflict.

My next adventure is a meeting with the consultant who has been hired to teach us about the new performance review and development program, an employee evaluation report. Why don't we call it what it is? I guess performance review sounds better, but I wonder if anyone really thinks the employees buy the wording. Everyone is embracing this "improved" method of evaluating performance. Is it really better? Or just different? Why are we changing? Its implementation is part of the latest answer to our management problems -- all we have to do is tie rewards (money) to performance. The concept makes sense; reward the people who perform the best -- how can you argue with that? It is apple pie and motherhood. My prejudices are showing; my heart is not in this. Why not? Perhaps it is because I came from an organization that spent millions, hundreds of millions, over the years attempting to develop an evaluation tool that would ensure the best were promoted. I personally lived through three iterations but the process never really changed -- promotions depended upon what your boss "thought" about your performance. The military raised this process to an art form but we were going to do it with eight hours of training; I think not. But how do you argue with a program that states the improved process is a mechanism for:

- setting performance standards,

- providing performance feedback,

- resolving performance problems,

- providing developmental opportunities,

- recognizing and rewarding performance.

Surely every manager and leader would support a program that provides that service. The program training book for supervisors describes the philosophy behind the program:

- fairness in performance management process is important;

- people want to know what is expected of them;

- people want ratings based on facts;

- good performance should be rewarded.

No one can argue with those objectives and since the public sector has demanded productivity, accountability, and a rating system that measures performance it seems like a logical step. After all, the ones who control the purse strings want the program. Now we have a system that meets those demands; let the money come. I'm being critical. Do I have a bad attitude? Why can't I see the benefit of this program? The first session ends and I leave with a knot in my stomach to accompany my headache. Why? I see the program unraveling. If the program is so good I wonder if there will be money allocated to reward good performance? Not likely; the proponents of the new evaluation system are not the ones who provide the funds, and attempts to provide "performance" funds in the budget have fallen short. There is not enough money to provide money to improve performance, yet improving performance is going to solve the problem of not having enough money. Catch 22, you can't get there from here; we are speaking out of both sides of our mouths. The employees' view? The ones I talk to are against it. They say it's unfair, that it will be too subjective, and that supervisors will play favorites, etc. There is something wrong here. These are all problems associated with the current system. What am I missing? The new system was designed to solve these problems.

On one hand, I believe any effort to "quantify" expectations is good. We should have ways to measure and reward performance and I know what a subjective system allows. But on the other hand, I can't come up with objective measures for "fostering teamwork." The proponents of measuring will come with some type of criteria but I don't believe it will work. Anything we come up with will boil down to a judgment call. Everyone I talk to agrees, but we are implementing the program anyway. We will have a new system. Is it nothing but a paperwork exercise? Will it really make a difference? But then, what difference are we looking for? If the new evaluation process satisfies the "system," thus allowing the system to move on to some other priority, is that success? Do we really know if it works? Do evaluation systems motivate employees? Are we evaluating what is really important or what we can easily measure? What do the employees think? Does that make a difference? To make matters worse, the Union has stepped in and we give everyone the same increase, but we still do the ratings. My foot slips off the rope for a minute but I take the next step, the next meeting.

I don't want to attend this meeting. I know where this one is heading. The conflict is guaranteed. The engineering solution is about to do battle with political reality; I know the outcome already. The capital budget submittal has been made but we have to "slip in" a $14 million electrical project "out of cycle." The questions are flying already. Why didn't we know about this earlier? How did you let this happen? You are the ones who are supposed to know about these things. Do you really want to know how we got here? I'll tell you again, even though I believe you know the answer. No, that will do no good. It will sound like whining. I see the sign over my boss's desk, "No Whining." As bad as this is, it gets worse. The engineers don't really know if $14 million is the correct cost. Are they guessing? No. It is an estimate; we told everyone that. We haven't designed the project. We don't even know where the project is to be sited so how can we know the costs? But we have to have a cost; the system demands it. We provided a budget number; it's in the program; the estimate is what people were told it will cost. Sure, we said it was an estimate, that the costs might grow, but no one heard that. The project has to be phased, says the planner. What do you mean, phased? It won't fit; we can't put $14 million in the program, is the reply. You have to split it up. What? We can't, is the engineer's response! We've put this project off for too long. The system is failing. In my heart I know what the engineers want. Their calculations are right, <u>but</u> they are conservative and if someone really pushed us we could do some "interim" fixes. But that approach is inefficient; it will create more work. If the project is delayed and if we don't have any "brown outs" over the summer, we will be told "we told you so; you engineers always cry wolf." Of course, if something does fail, it will be our fault. This is a no win -- for the engineer. Fourteen million dollars will not sell. We are going to have to change the project. The project does change and I have to peel the engineers off the ceiling. One of the engineers complains, "This is the way it has to be. You have to convince the 'powers.' That is your job!" I understand, but I wonder if anyone on the budget committee would like us to name an underground electrical cable after him? The project is phased and the estimate is revised (upwards) and the planners go nuts! You can't do that. We've told people the work will cost $14 million. If we tell them something else our credibility will be questioned. They won't believe anything we say; the project will be lost. I know they are right but I give my speech. We told you it was an estimate. Splitting it up costs more money. I go into overdrive. I get it off my chest and my boss smiles. He and I both know it will be phased but the original cost will be submitted. We'll do what we have to do. It won't be a good engineering solution. It will take me weeks to get the engineer in the right place. "If you are so good, you estimate the project," is their response. "We gave you the answer. Why can't you see the wisdom of our solution? You sold us out; you caved in," is what they say. No, I did not. The decision makers have a different perspective. They see a bigger picture. They have other battles to win. An electrical project is not high on their list. Maybe it should be but it isn't. The management books would suggest I explain this to the engineer. The books say if we work this as a team, they will understand. I try it but the engineers don't buy it. Now what do the management books suggest? Walk the tightrope. I move yet another step.

"I saved some money on the footings. But don't worry—no one will ever notice."

I return to my office and read the results of an employee survey that suggests the organization's climate needs to be improved. The report concludes that employees mistrust management. They feel all the emphasis on productivity is an attempt to get more work out of them, with no pay raises. They say we are threatening them with contracting out their jobs. Wait a minute. We've been told to involve them, to tell them what the problems are; let them help be part of the solution -- teamwork. I tell them we need to find better ways to do our jobs because of the competitive environment, but it comes back to me that we are threatening them. Something is wrong, but I understand where they are coming from. Some of them make $29,000 a year, work two jobs just to survive -- not live, but survive -- yet we expect them to see opportunities in this situation.

An employee comes to the office and wants a pay raise. "We haven't had a pay raise in five years and I need more money" is his rationale. He is not looking for a new job, or more responsibility, instead he wants his current job upgraded, reclassified. "I need a pay raise for retirement," he says. Not to do more for the organization, not as an incentive, but a reward for 27 years of service. "I can't do that," is my reply. "Why not? You have done it for others." Yes, but that was different; those jobs changed. "No, they haven't. They don't work as hard as I do; you're playing favorites; it's the 'good old boy' network; you do what the boss says and you get special treatment" is his response. The conversation goes downhill from there. My thoughts return to the employee survey: employees mistrust management; promotions are unfair; management doesn't support us. I wonder if this gentleman wrote any of those comments. The sad thing about this situation is that he is a hard worker. I remember when he was up to his waist in freezing water repairing a pipe. Ice was forming on his mustache and I had to order him out of the hole. I wonder if the new performance rating would let me rate him high enough to grant him a raise? Oh, I failed to mention, he was convicted of driving while intoxicated, yet I kept him on. Favoritism, no doubt. I bet the management books can tie a ribbon around this case. I take another step. I return to the stack of paper only to see a memo that describes a reduction in next year's budget. I understand why; I expected it; I can't argue it. Our budget is a logical target; we have has the largest "pot" of uncommitted money. We don't want to cut people; we don't want to cut programs; we don't want to delay making those facility repairs for one more year, but we can. My thoughts return to the professor who told the director that the solution to the HVAC problem required policy decisions and direction from his office. "I strongly believe your department has an obligation to both students and faculty to provide them with an atmosphere within which they can perform at their best." I wonder what he'd think if I told him the budget reduction just cut the project to fix his problem. Bet he'd say, "You have enough money, you people need to do your job."

What is blue and sleeps six? A Maintenance Truck. Eliminate all that waste and you'll have plenty of resources.

It's the end of the day and I never did check on the weird customer or the heating problem. No phone messages; I assume the heat is on. It wouldn't do any good to explain what happened anyway; move on. I didn't fall off the tightrope today; there were no serious problems; guess that's how I measure success.

Was what I described made up? No. Those are very typical problems, a very typical day. Are the events unusual? No. I've seen it; I've lived it; others have described it to me across the country and literally around the world. I know it is typical for an Air Force engineer; I know it is typical in higher education and in the public sector; and I suspect it is the same in the private sector, certainly according to Dilbert (Adams, 1996).

How do we deal with these conflicts, contradictions? Are the latest management philosophies the key? If so, how do I get the employees to buy in? It's not as easy as the textbooks would suggest. Are these techniques really different from the ones we've discarded in the past? Are Total Quality Management and Business Process Redesign really different from Management by Objectives, or the five steps of management that were taught 25 years ago: planning, organizing, coordinating, directing, and controlling? Those words sound harsh for an enlightened manager, but are things any different? Is it the "system" that is at fault? What is the system anyway, if it isn't us? Pogo said "We have met the enemy and he is us." Why do organizations do things that don't make sense? Why do organizations go on trips to Abilene (Harvey, 1988), why the Bay of Pigs, (Allison, 1971), why Vietnam (Janis, 1981)? Over the years I've seen organizations organize and then reorganize. Structures are changed; management philosophies come and go; yet the process remains the same. Is it just the nature of the business? Is it politics? Is it human nature?

Walking the Tightrope – On Several Levels

As we examine this world of middle management, we need to explore the three levels of contradictions. On the surface, balance is being maintained between the world of the customer and the world of the technicians, who in my case maintain the infrastructure, or in your case provides your service. In order to maintain some balance between the two, the middle manager must constantly manipulate the interface, to move back and forth, to build consensus, to build bridges.

Below the surface there is yet another world. This path has been shared by many over the years, as society debates the issues of management and leadership. What is the right way "to get things done through people" -- one definition of leadership. But how do you really define leadership? What is the difference between leadership and management? The popular notion is leadership is doing the right thing; management is doing things right. But I ask, isn't it important to do the right thing right? "We are lost but making great time" is no worse than "we are heading in the right direction but we will never get there." Volumes and volumes have been written about leadership and no one has come up with the "right" formula. On the management side of the fence, it's even worse. Management theories come and go like clockwork. The world, in which the middle manager works, declares that the current management philosophy has all the answers, and much time, energy and resources are applied to the latest theory.

Consultants are hired, teams are developed, plans are made...yet the same problems persist. Management has declared that numbers are important, accountability is necessary, and employees should be involved in the decision making process. Should one argue with those beliefs, those philosophies? Who would be against any of those things? Several years ago it was Theory X and Theory Y styles of leadership/management (McGregor, 1978). A Theory X manager believed you had to manipulate the employee; a Theory Y manager believed employees wanted to work, that employees were good. Who would admit to being a Theory X manager? Surely if an employee has a problem it is the "system's" fault, not the employee's. As the facility engineer contends with the desire to jump on the latest management bandwagon, because it is expected, because the people with the funds support it, he or she also has to deal with a reality that includes employees who have drug and alcohol addictions, others who make $29,000 a year, and still others who can neither read nor write. Employee development and employee involvement are sound theories but they run headlong into employees who view management with mistrust, and in some extremes, hatred. The world of management theories and practices has to be balanced with the realities of getting the job done. Charging the machine gun nest in war is not a task that suggests debate or consensus. Repairing a broken water main at 4 a.m. is not one either. Management philosophies come and go; getting the job done stays. It is easier to talk about how it should be done than it is to do it.

Finally, there is the third level, a more personal level--a world where I (and I assume others) find myself fighting a constant battle. This is the world that pits my outside being with my inner self. Each day walking the tightrope, staying on the path, requires an outward face that supports the customer, supports the common good at the expense of the individual, and does what the system expects because that is the job, the responsibility. But my inner self wants to throw it all to the wind, wants to get away from the constant need to put on yet another face. To survive in these worlds, and most certainly to be successful in these worlds, you have to constantly play the game, to be the politician, to work for the compromise, to accept that you are not the master of your own fate. As I started down this multi-level path so many years ago I took a test -- an Air Force Officers Qualifying Test. While it was an Air Force test, it was really a test that determined my life path. The type of questions? Would you rather be sitting on a mountain top playing a violin or working with a group to solve a problem? The right answer, the expected answer, the answer that determined my path was easy -- but I long for that mountain top. Maybe I feel this way because I'm getting older. Maybe it is time to move over (or is it out?). The critics will say I'm just bitter, that it is me. I don't think so; I've just kept it under wraps for all these years.

CHAPTER II
BEING A MIDDLE MANAGER

"Real leaders are ordinary people with
extraordinary determination."

Almost 40 years ago Peter Drucker (1974) suggested that all organizations, all companies, had to answer two basic questions in order to be successful; What is our business? and, Who are our customers? Over the years those questions have been asked in hundreds of different ways. Drucker's basic philosophy has been repackaged by thousands of consultants but is there really anything new? As an undergraduate student I learned that the tasks of a manager, a leader, (no distinction was made) were POCDC (planning, organizing, coordinating, directing, and controlling). From those basic functions we've moved through scientific management, the human relations movement, group dynamics, leadership theories, and even a contingency style of management was suggested as a way out of the management theory jungle (Koontz, 1978). Koontz's argument was quite simple, yet profound: "use what works." Along the way, any number of techniques, strategies, might I suggest fads, were proposed. Zero defects, management by objectives, theory X and Y and then theory Z styles of leadership, statistical quality control, critical path techniques, total quality management, quality control circles, T-groups, continuous improvement, and the latest concept, business process redesign, have all professed to be the answer, the solution to management problems. We discarded the scientific method, only to discover the human relations method. We discarded management and found leadership. A trip to a bookstore in the 1990-92 timeframe would lead you to hundreds of books on leadership, one even suggesting that Attila the Hun (Roberts, 1985) had the answers. A trip in 1998 lead you to hundreds of books on strategic planning, business process redesigned, and other process related topics, all professing to be the answer. A trip in 2007 finds more of the same, to include all kinds of books on how to manage your "inner self."

As I searched through the literature, as I looked for the right path, the right technique, I discovered that what sounded good in theory, what seemed to make sense, didn't work very well in the "real world." The real world was much more complicated, much more complex, than the theories would suggest. The environment, the players pulling on the rope, their interactions, and their conflicting goals and objectives generate many realities and I find myself asking: "Where is this real world?" One cannot begin to understand the forces that influence the middle manager until you look beyond the day-to-day events that seem to consume their time and energy. While these problems frustrate me, I must admit I am most comfortable on the surface. Give me a problem to solve; I will marshal the resources. I will get the job done, but I know that solving the air-conditioning problem is the easiest part. The human side of the equation is the most difficult to understand. On the surface, there is the constant struggle between responding to the customer and being sensitive to the needs, desires, and complaints of those who work for me. After I was hired for my current position, I found that the supervisors who would be working for me wanted another. I discovered they didn't believe I would support them, protect them, keep the customer at arm's length. My predecessor was one of them; he had come up through the ranks, he had been here for 30 years. He defended them; he kept others away from them, so they wanted another him. On the other side of the coin, the customers had also chosen another. They didn't believe I could understand their needs, their requirements. I was not one of them. As time passed, I won over the customers. Have I won over the supervisors? I don't know. The new ones, perhaps; the old ones, I doubt it.

The surface is a world of organizational structures, wiring diagrams, of reporting officials, of conflicting goals and objectives, of various agendas. It involves a lot of politics, bureaucracy, and emphasis on objectivity and rationality. But what is rational? Is what is good for the community, good for the individual? While the policy makers balance the conflicting goals and try to meet the needs of the many, I am pouring concrete. The world of industry in general and the public sector in particular, is difficult to describe. The public sector is often considered a bureaucracy that is non-responsive and filled with lazy, do-nothing public servants. While I have seen some of those, my experience tells me most want to do a good job but rules, regulations, and policies govern their actions. However, I must be careful. I don't want to fall into the trap that supports the assertion that the system is at fault. Give people authority and power and the ineffectiveness, the red tape of government, will be eliminated is the cry of the reformers. But we don't want that. A democracy-- our society-- is designed to be inefficient and checks and balances are what make it work, admittedly slowly and with considerable waste, but it does what it was designed to do . . . it prevents a powerful force from driving the agenda. Bailey (1978) describes this environment in his essay: <u>The Peculiar Mixture:</u> <u>Public Norms and Private Space</u> "In a generic sense, our society is trying to sort out what all generations of free people must sort out: that peculiar mixture of freedom and order that is compatible with evolving norms of social justice on one hand

and with fostering of both critical and creative impulses on the other . . . the eternal yin and yang of democratic politics the need to promote equity without destroying individuality, the need to satisfy claims of fairness without stultifying essential life forces."

The world of the public sector, higher education, and, I would argue, the private sector as well consists of multiple goals, objectives, and priorities. Birnbaum (1988) describes four worlds in one when he looks at institutions of higher education: a collegial world, one governed by group norms and consensus; a bureaucracy, a world of rules, regulations, and policies; a political world, a world of power; and finally an organized anarchy, a world of decentralization, mixed signals, and unclear technology. While much of the literature studies the academic side of the enterprise and concurs with Birnbaum's analysis, most suggest that the support activities (the physical plant being one of the largest) should adhere to business practices and be measured by efficiencies and effectiveness (Massey & Wilger, 1992). While I would agree there are many "business activities" on this side of the street (bills are paid, the grass is cut, and supplies are ordered), I wonder why so many suggest that efficiency and effectiveness should be the norm? The customers are quick to criticize but they don't realize their conflicting goals and objectives influence this side of the enterprise. Our inefficiencies, our mistakes, are easy to point out. Everyone who has ever driven a nail or painted a room is an expert but the customers do not understand. Perhaps they don't want to, or need to, but if they are going to criticize, if they are going to tell me how I should do my job, they need to walk in our shoes for a while.

The conflicting goals, the political decisions create nothing but frustration for most, if not all, managers. If you pick the system apart, it is hard to explain why individual problems aren't solved. I cannot tell the professor, who returns from sweating through a lecture, that there is not enough money to fix the HVAC system. If there is enough money to paint buildings, cut grass, and send people to conferences, I can't find an argument that is going to make any sense to him. If we made his number one priority our number one priority, his problem would be fixed. A meeting with the faculty of the School of Music highlights my dilemma. Their building has reached the end of its life expectancy and chilled water lines are so clogged that water cannot get through them. I don't care how much we tinker with the system it will not work very well. But who cares? Be assured a musician sweating through a performance doesn't care about the reason; get it fixed is the demand. It is my problem; I'm supposed to support his needs. It's my problem, not his! But I can only plead with the technicians, jury-rigging the system is our only recourse. We fix it today but it is out of control. If it gets cold tomorrow, the faculty will be freezing and we will be back tinkering again. Meanwhile, as we fix this problem someone else will be complaining that we have not fixed his. It is not a case of not getting complaints; it is a case of who is going to complain.

On the other side, it isn't any easier. The technicians want to know why they aren't getting paid more; they want to know why new buildings are built and old ones are not maintained. They want me to tell the customers we aren't going to jump through hoops to address their every complaint. The customers don't understand, they don't care, and all they do is make demands, is the technician's argument. While there is certainly some truth in this perspective, I don't want to overreact. We receive as many positive notes as bad ones, but it seems that one "Ah shucks" wipes out one hundred "Atta boys!"

While many call for change, the conflicting goals are a real deterrent to "major" overhauls in how we do business. Being efficient, the elimination of non-value-added steps, increasing productivity, and a host of other goals are heralded as the answer, but I've lived through too many solutions to be anything but cynical. In fact, in many cases we've come full circle. We are where we were

35 years ago. We are back to the beginning. What we changed did not work, so we are changing again. Of course we changed the first time because what we had done before (what we are going to do again) didn't work. Confused? So am I. I'm tired of chasing my tail -- we rearrange things, we declare success, but we never really change. Yet, as soon as I give my pessimistic speech, I tell myself -- quit being so negative. Change is constant. One person can make a difference. Organizations do take on the characteristics of those who are leading them (Kotter, 1990). Perhaps change is incremental, perhaps the best we can do is keep the herd heading in the right direction while keeping most close to the same path. Maybe the calf knew what he was doing after all. Perhaps our mistake is in following, the blind acceptance and not questioning. Can a leader or a manager really make a difference? Are the other forces doing the leading? The management and leadership models that have influenced my journey are numerous and varied, but they all seem to heighten my frustration. Nonetheless, there are several that I come back to time and time again -- they help me make sense of the complexities, the contradictions I face every day.

The first is the work of Bolman and Deal (1984). Their organizational frames of reference suggest that one's view of the world influences, if not dictates, how one reacts to a given situation, to a given set of circumstances. I find that as I dwell in the structural frame, others see my actions through a human relations, political, or symbolic frame. Reflecting on these views of the world helps me understand the complexities of trying to make the right decision. Second is the work of Allison (1971) and his analysis of decision making. Here again, one's perspective, one's view of the world, and one's objectives have an impact on one's actions. A rational decision, one that weighs the alternatives against some well-defined, quantifiable criteria, will lead to one conclusion. However, a decision based on a political agenda will lead to a different conclusion; the same reality is viewed differently. But is a decision truly rational if it doesn't deal with all the agendas? Third is the work of Birnbaum (1988) and others who have characterized the world of higher education as a mixture, a conglomerate, of many worlds dwelling in the same space. This view helps explain why staying on an even keel is so difficult. Fourth is Morris Massey's (1979) thesis: "What you are (is determined by) where you were when." His analysis of why people react differently to the same environment is based on his theory that one's personality, one's concept of the world, is established at about the age of ten. His examples, his arguments, have helped me see that differences in age are more than just a physical characteristic. Finally, I reflect on some of the classic organization theorists, the writings of Maslow and McGregor, philosophies that are ageless and continue to influence my questioning. I recall the lectures of Professor Rich Johnson, the lone civilian on the teaching staff at the Air Force Institute of Technology's Civil Engineering School. Rich took a group of young captains under his wing and taught us there was more than a technical approach to the world. I will never forget his lecture entitled: "Happiness is a Warm Six Pack." Based on the writings of Graves (1970) he described the different types of people within a facility maintenance organization with humor and great insight.

Although all of these theories, models, approaches to leadership and management influence my thinking and help explain the reasons for my frustration, they provide me little comfort. They all point out the complexities of managing and leading; they all tell me about the difficulties I will encounter, but they do not provide the answer I am looking for. Perhaps there is no answer; perhaps all one can hope for is understanding. Few have ventured into the world of understanding. Even fewer have explored the relationships in order to see how people work below the surface, to see if what happens is the same as what is advertised. Bilello (1993) took a very unique look at a process that should be a classic example of rational decision making -- building a building. When he looked at the process through the lens of Bolman and Deal, (1984) he found a much different environment and concluded that one's frame of reference changes a very concrete process into one of multiple, conflicting concepts and ideas. This process created, along with the building, conflicts, inefficiencies, and uncertainty. The building ended up costing much more than the construction cost, costs that were more than dollars and cents. Some saw the process through the structural frame and were concerned about the bricks and steel. Others dealt with relationships; others made political deals and power brokering was the norm; still others saw the building through what it symbolized, the actual structure was not very important. His analysis was extremely insightful. On one plane, people were proud of what the building represented. On another, some were proud of what the building symbolized, but I saw the process as nothing but conflict. The surface looked good but what was going on behind the scenes? Did it matter to the one who cut the ribbon on opening day? I doubt it. Does it matter to the one who is going to get blamed when something about the building doesn't work, even if he had nothing to do with how it was built? You can count on it. But this perspective is not heard, or if heard, it is not a priority. The short-term perspective costs money in the long run but that is on someone else's watch; short-term objectives and limited resources seem to drive the decisions (Meisinger, 1994; Schmidtlein, 1990). Don't tell me how it should be done -- I deal with how it is done -- and it is done that way over and over again. Why can't I simply apply what I've been taught? There are many telling me how to do things, many quoting the latest management technique, but all I see is repackaging. Is there nothing new? Is there an answer? Just get on with the job, is my cry. Am I practicing Theory X management? Is it a self-fulfilling prophecy? No, it is reality, I tell myself, but then, what is reality? Does your world behave like the "rational" model would suggest?

You are told not to be a yes man, but to support the organization's objectives. While the easy retort is: "You have to decide when to fall on your sword," I cannot mix what is easy to say with what is hard to do. I have learned that lesson well. A commander wanted a project done and looked to two subordinates to make it happen. One quoted the rules and told him why it couldn't be done. There was no question about it - - the rules, rightly or wrongly, said not to do it. The other one found a way. He bent the rules, he redefined the rules, he made up new rules and got it done. The can-do, problem solving one got promoted, the other did not. If the decision is ever questioned I wonder if the commander will support the can-do, problem-solver, or will he say: "I didn't tell him to do that." This is not an isolated incident; it is not unique to the military; it happens every day, in this business and I'm sure in others. The promotion was deserved, but it was tainted, and I will never forget the experience, I was the one who found a way. As I'm challenged to be more business-like and to increase productivity, the tools to effect the change are hard to find. Who can argue with the objectives: be more competitive, reward people for performance, do strategic planning, think long term. We can improve, we are improving. The stacks of reports and claims of increased productivity sound good, but are they over-stated? What is the real objective? Perhaps the symbolic successes are what we are looking for, but we sold the programs to the employees using a different argument. I'm in the middle and it is hard to balance so many agendas.

To be successful you have to play both ends against the middle. You have to constantly shift priorities, balance, cajole, plead, and threaten. But this isn't what the management books suggest. Get the employees involved, get them to buy in is the argument. But what if my objective is not theirs? Can I change their objectives? Many would say yes, but I haven't been very successful. I continue to ask myself, is it me? Why can't I use the management techniques I've been taught? Stop being negative, I tell myself. We are a team. We can all get ahead, but then I deal with an engineer who complains that his boss always has to have it his way. I spend hours explaining that he has to see the bigger picture, but the engineer says I'm not supporting him. We are not communicating. What are the many forces influencing the manager and their ability to stay balanced and focused on the task at hand? Which of these forces, and your management of them, will determine your success or failure?

"We cannot direct the wind but we can adjust the sails."

CHAPTER III
THE REALITIES OF MIDDLE MANAGEMENT

I find that those who want to tell us how to "fix" the shortcomings of our world fail to grasp its complexity, the magnitude of the issues, or the art that is the science. As efforts to quantify the work environment expand, there is a demand to be more performance-oriented. Measure results and pay for performance is the cry, but what results are we looking for? The demand is not new, I've heard it for years but demanding it and getting it are two different things. As long as the customers don't complain, as long as the employees aren't "up in arms," I can be in control of my destiny. But once a customer gets frustrated enough to go over my head, it takes a great deal of effort to get the system back in equilibrium. If the employees decide to take their complaints outside the organization, my priorities are changed.

As I share my frustrations with those I have worked for, their frustrations reverberate back; it is as if I were looking in a mirror. They sympathize a little, empathize a small amount, but ultimately they tell me to rise above the conflict. They say they understand the pressures, the conflicts, the contrasting priorities, but I don't think they really understand. I am often told I need to spend more time on the bigger issues, on long-term strategies, on programs that the "system" believes need to be emphasized: productivity, accountability, and a more external focus. I wonder why, why this emphasis? The response often is: budget pressures, increasing expectations, reduced resources, an audit report that suggests, no, <u>says</u>, our controls are weak and that management isn't "managing," i.e., keeping track of how efficient we are. The report suggests our system can't determine whether the employees are "taking advantage" of us. How do you reconcile that perspective with the one that tells me to empower the employee, to cut down on controls, to reduce paperwork? I know, I know, we need the proper amount of control, but who determines what is proper?

Did these problems just materialize? Are these issues really that important, or are they just the ones that are the current emphasis? I look back over my forty-plus years and they are the same issues. I recall my days at the "worst" base in England. As I was preparing to leave after three years of an all-consuming effort, I was proud of what we had accomplished. As I toured with the new base commander and my replacement, it was obvious that they saw all the things that weren't done. They were coming from a world that was much better and they saw what was bad. I was coming from three years earlier and saw what was improved. The new commander said his people didn't deserve to have facilities like this and they were going to turn the place around. I should have smiled knowingly. I should have understood their perspective, but I was tired. I was tired of being "beat up." I was tired of being pushed to bend the rules. I was tired of three years without a break. I was tired and wasn't going to listen to someone who had all the answers, but didn't even know the question. It is not a question of being yelled at; it's just a question of who is going to be yelling about what.

Perhaps the complexity of our job is in its simplicity. Can we accept the fact that we can't do all things for all people? Can we accept the fact that we typically respond to those who complain and deal with what's hot? Can we accept the fact that while we are doing a job in one area, others are waiting and they are the ones who are going to feel shortchanged? The have-nots will fight to gain ground and the haves will fight to stay where they are; when you are dealing with limited resources it is inevitable. You can't win; win-win is a myth. While you are responding to one problem, you are not responding to another. The customers and executives of any organization want to know what's going on; they want answers so they can make decisions. Whether it's a resources allocation decision, a decision to close school because of bad weather, a decision to renovate an office, a question of when a project will be complete so follow-on decisions can be made; everyone wants to know the facts. Their frustration with me and with the system is apparent. When will the power be restored? When will the roads and parking lots be cleared of snow? How much will the project cost? When will it be done? Our bosses expect us to know the answers and then expect us to make it happen. The examples of this reality are everywhere.

As I read The Nightingale's Song (Timberg, 1995), trying to grasp an understanding of the influence of power in the public sector, I ran across yet another example of the frustrations. The following is but a brief interlude in John Poindexter's journey, but it struck a chord – a brief glance at the "system's" view of our world. As chief engineer, he (Poindexter) held the most responsible position on the ship after the captain and the executive officer. If the chief engineer doesn't perform, toilets don't flush, showers don't work, guns don't turn, and the ship doesn't sail. Many engineering officers begin to think their first names have been changed to damn it, because the captains always shouting, "Damn it, Mr. So-and-So, what the hell's wrong with my ship?" We can't escape our lot in life.

The criticisms mount. Some of the comments are good-natured, but after you hear them over and over again they get old and one becomes defensive. "Why are there three men standing over the hole while only one is working?" I am asked. I've been asked that question and variations of it a hundred times and have heard the joke, "how many maintenance men does it take to (fill in the blank)" thousands of times over the years. Those who criticize, those who think they can do better, don't think twice about spending several hours in a meeting, yet a meeting over the hole is ripe for a jab.

What are the realities that govern the world of middle management? More importantly what will be your response to those realities?

Black and White Versus All Gray

We would all like the world to be black and white, yes or no, the right way or the wrong way, true or false, for any x there is only one y. Unfortunately that is not the way it is, in fact, in the world of management I would argue there is nothing but gray; judgment and problems with no answers are the norm. Granted there are some certainties, i.e. economic reorder points and profit and loss statements, but if you fall prey to the belief that you can prove things with data (I can prove most things if you allow me to "select" my sample, pick my parameters), if you believe everyone will see your side if you just explain it to them, you are in trouble.

One is expected to be consistent, fair (or equal), and to know the answers, but in reality you need to be flexible, you need to work the system, you need to support the people who are going to be there when you need them. What sounds good in theory, doesn't work well in practice.

Marry Not An Engineer

Verily I say unto you, marry not an engineer; for the
engineer is a strange being possessed by many devices;
yea, he speaketh in parables which he calleth formulae,
and he wieldeth a big stick which he calleth a slide rule;
he hath but one bible -- his handbook.

He talketh away of stresses and strains and of no end of thermodynamics; he showeth always a serious aspect and seemeth not to know how to smile; and he picketh his seat on the car by the number of springs therein and not by the damsel thereon. Neither does he know a waterfall except for its power, not a sunset but for its specific heat.

Always he carrieth books with him and he entertaineth his maiden with steam tables. Verily, though the damsel expecteth chocolates, when he calleth, he opens the package to reveal samples of a new alloy.

Yea, he holdeth a damsel's hand, but only to measure the friction, and he kisseth only to test viscosity. For in his eye shineth a faraway look which is neither love nor longing, but a vain attempt to remember an equation.

Even as a little boy, he pulleth a girl's hair but to test its elasticity, and as a man he discovereth different devices, for he would hold a maiden to his bosom only to count the palpitations of her heart, and to record the strength of her material.

Alas! His marriage is a simultaneous equation, involving two unknowns and yielding a periodic function.

- Author Unknown

The poem is a little outdated, the slide rule has been replaced by a calculator, but it does hold some truths. Unfortunately the world we live in will challenge everything a lot of us hold dear. The conflicting goals and objectives, the complex interactions, and the rational in competition with the non-rational all demand the ability to walk the tightrope. Do not expect black or white. It is very easy to recite the rules, it is easy to say everyone should be treated the same, given the same opportunities but there are many factors that influence the interface between customers and producers, with the middle manager stuck in the middle.

Perhaps the most disturbing reality is the feeling of powerlessness, on all sides. We all know what we want to be done, but doing it is the problem. The customer feels that the physical plant, or any service organization, is a monolithic organization, a giant at the end of the service desk that responds to no one, that does what it wants to do, that moves only when prodded, when forced by an important face. The professor calls the Dean, asking for action. "It seems that something gets done only when <u>you</u> ask for it." The professor who expects policy decisions doesn't know who makes those decisions, or how to influence the system but he wants <u>someone</u> to do it. Even my bosses have expressed frustration over their inability to get "us" to do what they want. Equally as frustrated are the employees. They believe I have the power to do whatever I want. If I wanted to, I could promote them; if I wanted to, I could make the system respond; if I wanted to, I could solve their problems. In some instances their perception is correct. I have a tremendous amount of power, and this is not an egotistical claim. While there are controls, while there are limits; I have a lot of influence in the process. I can't determine when a new building gets built, but I do influence the process and I can focus a lot of resources. I can get a customer's office cooled. I can get his office painted. I can get an employee reclassified (within reason). I can influence how hundreds of thousands of dollars are spent. I can get a response out of a 1000-person workforce. Because of my personality, my make-up, I can make it happen. However, I have limits. As I shed my tie and don jeans to help shovel snow, a member of the community comes up and yells -- "Why can't you get this sidewalk cleaned any faster? I don't have any boots on. Your bosses ought to do something to make it get done faster." People are the same everywhere. This is not unique. After the numerous computer messages, I want to find a person at the end of that telephone line. The feeling of powerlessness is all-consuming.

As people react to their inability to influence the systems around them, they seem to say – "I have no power, no ability to influence; therefore I have no responsibility for making it better -- that is your job." All are more than willing to give me their problems. Common refrains are recorded over and over again: "I don't have the resources to do the job." "I'm not paid to do the job." "The rules don't let me do it." "It's not my responsibility; it's yours." "The system is the problem, you fix it." Unfortunately, most fixes require judgments, require questioning the rules. While rules are there to prevent abuses, they are made by mere mortals. A previous boss used to make the following comparison between public law and rules and policies: "Don't mess with public law, even if it is bad, but rules and policies are written by people like you and me. Policies are great for guidelines, but they can't deal with every issue, they shouldn't be used as something to hide behind. You have to do what you think is right but then, you have to be prepared to live with those who will second-guess you. It is easy to give advice, but it is hard to make the call."

As I reflect on that perspective, I turn to Workman (1992) and her experience with policy-making. As a social worker, she sees her world as two realities: the reality of human connectedness with people in a helping relationship, and the reality of an organizational world of policies and procedures. She finds herself wrestling with the words of policy and the experience of living within its framework. She finds that policies, designed to give orderliness to action, cannot ease the pain, the wonder, the awe, the hopefulness, and the experience of living it. Policy is supposed to provide answers, bring clarity to confusion, and to tell us what to do, but it does not provide understanding. Lindblom (Bennveniste, 1989) notes that policies need to be bent if they do not work well, and that policy must be a guiding light, one that can create an aura of comfort and direction, but one that can also be used to find a new direction. I agree with that perspective and embrace it, but I, like Workman, find that challenging policy is an uncertain experience. Policy can be a crutch, an excuse for staying the course, and people tend to support policy when it supports their objectives, but criticize it when it doesn't. Workman concludes that policy requires interpretation, and yet there is a sense of breaking a rule for which something dreadful results. Why do I feel comfortable challenging the rules and others hide behind them? But then, this practice frequently gets me into trouble. I am told to treat everyone the same, but there is no same situation. I am told to follow the rules, but I am expected to get the job done. The customers want us to be responsive; the auditor wants us to have controls. I am told to staff my work centers with people who only possess an eighth grade education, yet everyone wants us to empower our employees. I'm sorry; I don't have the power to be all things to all parties.

Everyone I talked to, every management book I've read, and every consultant I ever met stressed the importance of communication, but do we want communication or answers? The customer wants to know the status of his or her job. When will it be fixed? Why can't the problem go away? Why is it even here? Who is going to solve my problem, and when is the work going to be done?" That is the information they want. Their requests are understandable but many times I don't have the answer. Meanwhile, the employees want to know what their future is going to be like. They want to know why things happen the way they do. They want to know why such "dumb" decisions are made. How do I answer these questions? The management books say I'm supposed to communicate, to "explain the facts." I'm told that if I answer the question "they" will understand. But many times I can't provide an answer. Many questions don't have answers; some have answers but I can't share them; others have answers that some don't want to hear; some answers aren't the right ones no matter what. One doesn't say "your priority just isn't very important," or, "the organization isn't going to solve your problem." That is pretty crass but it can be the reality. I find the "politically correct" way to say it, I qualify my answer.

I tell them we'll work on it, and then I wonder if they accept or understand what I said. In most cases they will say that I'm not really answering the question, or that I'm not being honest, or even worse, they only hear the part they want to hear. I am told I am vague, that I'm wishy-washy, and that I "play to the audience." I guess I'm guilty, but it is the only way to stay in control. That is not a very admirable posture, but it is one that provides space to maneuver. It helps one stay on the tightrope.

It's been two years since the professor wrote his letter and nothing has changed from his vantage point. Another season will pass and he'll be just as hot. How do I tell him his priority isn't high enough? It's the system's problem, but I'm the face of the system. Mine is the face he sees; the rest of the system is faceless. We all want someone to be responsible. People want answers; that's their real definition of communication. We have become enamored with data, with instant information, but neither is "communication." We do not, cannot, solve issues to everyone's satisfaction so we tailor our responses, we word things very carefully; we do what needs to be done to support the current agenda. Why am I surprised when people pick the part they want to hear and discard the rest?

Everyone wants clear cut decisions, everyone wants answers. It seems that the "answer" to most of our problems is to communicate. People will understand, they will support the decision if you explain the reasons for your position. The management consultants say we all want the same thing; we all want and support the "mission" of our organization. At the strategic level it probably works, we all want the company to be the best; we all want to be number one but when you get to the world of limited resources, when you get to conflicting priorities it all falls apart.

- Cut the budget, but don't cut my program.

- Fix the leaky pipe, but don't impact me.

- Reduce the number of utility outages but don't raise the rates.

We want answers, we want things to be easy, we want our problems solved, and we want our life to be easier. All understandable wants, all unrealistic expectations, and none of it is new.

The More Things Change - The More They Stay The Same

As I reflect on my pessimism, I review a scrapbook of articles from the early 1980s, a scrapbook maintained by a department secretary. The articles suggest that the issues we are dealing with are not new, they are in fact universal and continuing. Article after article describes budget cuts, energy problems, concerns about asbestos and PCBs, staff shortages, and concerns about low pay. Those articles could have been written today; the only difference is the PCB articles would be replaced by concerns about indoor air quality and sick building complaints. One article in 1983 told customers that a new computer system was going to improve the slow response to service calls. We are making those same claims today.

An editorial in the campus newspaper echoes complaints I've heard for years and declares: "Physical Plant, the name sends cold chills from the nape of one's neck to the tip of one's big toe. Ah yes, Physical Plant, sometimes referred to as 'those jerks,' is responsible for the upkeep and maintenance of our wonderful campus. This is ridiculous. Something must be done about Physical Plant. I mean, it is obvious that the bureaucracy there has its priorities more than a little messed up."

An article from 1980 notes that the carpenters filed a grievance charging that they were underpaid and that much of the work they do is too menial for their abilities. They argue that although the University granted a pay raise, the carpenters did not receive fair treatment because some shops received a two or three grade raise while they only received one. A carpenter complains: "For me, it's not so much the money that I am after by backing the grievance, it is the pride that I have in my trade as a carpenter" (School newspaper, Sept. 17, 1980). I would like to believe it but I heard those exact statements in reaction to the new pay plan in 1996 and in 2008. I know many say money doesn't motivate, but it sure dominates discussions. The point/ counterpoint continued in 1981 and the workers planned a job action during the fall registration, to protest a $15 parking fee and the denial of the cost-of-living pay raise. Although the scheduled sick-out was declared a failure by the administration, the union declared victory. "The administration has had to take notice that employees on the campus are not satisfied." (School newspaper, July 30, 1981). In 1996 they still weren't satisfied. 2007 was not much better, just different people and we are dealing with the same issues in 2012.

Although the issues of the early 1980s could easily be transposed to the late 1990s, there was another interesting facet of my look at the past. Names of current employees jumped off the page and I found people have been saying the same things, have been doing the same things, for 15 years. For one who has moved around, performed a variety of tasks, and seen facility maintenance organizations literally around the world, this look of stability raises a new perspective. In 1981, an article quoted a Physical Plant employee: "We want the University to give us a decent wage. If we don't get $2000 there will be no steam." (School newspaper, July 30, 1981). This same employee has been a constant source of frustration over the last several years as he questions every decision, as he argues that the employees aren't being treated fairly. Another article describes how an employee was airlifted to a hospital after a steam line he was working on ruptured, scalding his face and arms. This employee has become a vocal critic of the organization, but he does his job. What is his motivation? What does he expect from me? He mistrusts management. What does he want?

This look back is comforting on one hand but very disturbing on the other. It is comforting in the sense that the issues that consumed me in the early 1980s are the same in 2001, and today. However, it is disturbing in the sense that issues don't go away; problems are not solved, they just go underground for a while. I reflect back to 1971, my first job in a facility maintenance organization, when I was asked to improve service and increase the productivity of our exterior electricians, our linemen. This group was notorious for doing "nothing" all day, but few saw them at 2 a.m. in the morning climbing ice-covered power poles with a wind chill factor of 40 below. What is a measure of their productivity? What do we want these people to do? I've gone through dozens of management models over the years, all designed to improve performance, all designed to solve this problem, but what is the problem? Maybe, just maybe, all one can do is understand the issue, understand the relationships; perhaps solving it is not possible. That revelation is very disturbing; I'll never get off this path. The issues remain the same today. People seem to be constantly complaining about poor service from the federal government, the local government, their schools, their service providers, from everyone.

On the other hand, there is no question there has been tremendous change over the years. I don't want to fall into the trap of "it has always been that way and won't change" but I don't want to be naive and say "we can make all these problems go away." We have to acknowledge change is constant, technology continues to improve and new challenges come up, but the people issues don't change, the conflicting goals and objectives remain. That is a reality we better be prepared to deal with.

Conflicting Goals and Objectives

As I try to deal with the reality of conflicting goals and objectives, the different perspectives, and the inability to reconcile management theory with practical realities, I turn to that basic belief -- you have to walk the walk before you can talk the talk; don't tell me how to do it unless you have done it. To truly understand the dynamics of this or any business one has to understand the three distinct worlds: the world of the customers, the world of the service provider, and the world of the "outsiders," the ones who impact the interface. The goals and objectives of each of these groups are different, and often compete (Austin & Klein, 1996). However, there is more to the relationships than just the physical space these groups occupy. For example, Birnbaum (1988) notes that higher education has no one common goal or objective and instead there are competing "worlds" within this world. Equally as important, the Physical Plant includes a number of competing worlds (Haggans, 1995). The engineers look at a task one way; the trades look at the same task in another way. All of these players interact on different planes. The physical worlds are different; the way they view what is important is different; they are living and working in different places. In order to truly understand the role of the middle manager one must gain an understanding of these worlds and how they interact.

However, these different worlds are but one factor that separates the engineers, the organization, from the mainstream. The engineer speaks another language and often has a problem explaining a problem or a solution in layman's terms. Engineers are seldom schooled in anything but technical courses and often find themselves like fish out of water when they have to write something other than a technical report, speak in an environment other than their own, or present ideas rather than facts. These characteristics separate; they do not pull together. From an organizational perspective, the trades do not interact very well with the client, the customer. Although technically competent, they often lack a "political view" and some, even in a college environment, have only very basic reading and writing skills. Place one of these individuals in a confrontation with a professor whose air conditioner doesn't work and the outcome is predictable. In addition, these individuals have historically been told what to do. They were given little latitude to make decisions by themselves and were told that the best way to respond to a problem was to do only what they had been told. It's safer to buck decisions to their supervisors. You can find yourself in less trouble if you simply do what you are told. It's someone else's responsibility to make the decision.

Within any organization there are conflicts, different goals and objectives, different perspectives and there seem to be the age old stereotypes of "blue" collar and "white" collar workers. In maintenance organizations this division is reinforced as engineers, who learn their "trade" in college, interact with technicians who have years of experience in the field. The technicians suspect the engineer because he/she doesn't know how to fix the equipment, yet they make the "big" bucks. A facility engineer who can bridge the division between those who work on the equipment and those who design the equipment is a rare breed. To earn the respect of the crusty, weather-beaten plumber is indeed a chance occurrence. Is there any question of why a balancing act is required?

As noted earlier, the engineer sees his world, and the world around him/her as black or white; structure, rational and quantifiable decision making, and formulas are key. Engineering solutions are predictable, are right; there is no reason to modify a solution to a problem. On the other hand, the world in which he/she deals consists of multiple frames and conflicting, but equally important, values. The decision-making and resource allocation process has to balance conflicting priorities, has to apply limited resources to the most pressing needs, and the allocation is seldom made in a rational, i. e. strictly quantifiable, manner (Layzell & Lyddon, 1993). The priorities do not line up; they can't, but the engineers are expected to establish funding priorities even though the facilities support conflicting objectives. The rational decision, from an economic point of view, would be to fund that electrical upgrade project as a single contract. The project would be easier to design; it would cost less in the long run; it would solve some serious "engineering" problems. But that won't happen. The budget process will reign supreme. The conflicting priorities, taking political, social, and other non-economic variables into consideration, and the many organizational structures complicate the decision making and resource allocation processes. While all will argue that they appreciate the importance of the facilities that support their mission, I believe, if they are honest, they will acknowledge they would rather leave those decisions to someone else (Mintzberg, 1979). Since there is no profit or loss statement in the public sector, it is easy to understand why activities that aren't directly related to the objectives, the mission of the organization, are left to the "support" activities. Who is the person or process responsible for lining up all these conflicting goals and objectives and determining which one is indeed number one? What do you mean you don't know who is going to be occupying the building but you want a cost estimate for the building modifications? I know where this is leading me. I can't tell you how much it is going to cost until you tell me what the requirements are. If I give you a number it will be cast in concrete. If I change it, it will be too late; the money will be appropriated based on our wild guess and we will be stuck with it. Don't tell me you know it's an estimate; I've been burned too many times before. The earlier electrical upgrade example is but one of many. Once the project is authorized/appropriated, it is unlikely that anyone is going to go back and ask for more money; the project would be put in jeopardy. Don't worry will be the response, we'll get it started; we know we aren't getting the best, but it's better than nothing. Don't tell me that. Next year when it doesn't work no-one will remember we "bought in" on the cheap.

That conversation goes on continually as maintenance organizations compete in the political arena and limited resources are spread around conflicting and competing programs. That is the way it has to be, but there are those who argue that the facilities business has to act in a rational manner, in a supposedly non-rational environment. How do you make rational decisions in a world that doesn't live by mathematical models, by cost/benefit analysis? Can you make a rational decision? What, in fact, is rational? To complicate an already complicated environment, politics are found at every level and influence virtually every decision in the public sector. Whether one likes it or not, political decisions are a way of life. While there are all kinds of stories, as well as any number of truths about "pork barrel" projects (Choate, 1981), political decisions and politics often gets an undeserved bad rap. The art of compromise, of negotiation, of providing just enough funds to sustain a program for another year, are all legitimate ways to allocate resources. With the conflicting priorities, with needs that far exceed resources, with special groups with special needs, and society's shifting priorities there is little question about the importance of resource allocation decisions. Keeping everything balanced, or at least trying to, is the challenge. Unfortunately, in the facilities business this often equates to save in the short run, spend even more in the long run. Of course, as the old saying goes: "You will never see a politician who will reduce spending in his/her district with some promise that it will increase funding in the future. After all, they probably won't be around to live with the results."

A university, any organization, has to move in many circles, in many worlds, and has conflicting needs, all competing for the same funding. An understanding of the methods used to make those decisions is critical if a manager is going to be successful. There is a wealth of literature that tells the facility engineers how they should do their job, how they need to "justify" their requirements (Dillon, 1986); but few, if any, of the experts deal with the realities. An important aspect of this world is the age old problem of short-term versus long-term objectives. The political process, by its very nature, forces an organization to "think" short term as budget decisions are made on a yearly basis, as priorities change and emphasis shifts to meet political needs. Nonetheless, most of the recent management theories argue that strategic planning and the development of vision statements allow organizations to look long term (Benvennte, 1989), but in reality, many organizations spend hours on analysis and nothing is resolved. These two ends of the balance bar are problematic. For example, a facility master plan is designed to stabilize land use planning, site buildings, establish the utility infrastructure, and lay out transportation systems, but shifting priorities move buildings around the map. Doing master planning on a piece of paper is much different than laying cable in the ground. The engineers are often criticized for not anticipating problems with the infrastructure and utilities, but the priorities keep changing. As the budget requests move forward the questions are asked. Why didn't you think about this earlier? Now it is an emergency. Why didn't you plan ahead? Stop. If you look back in the capital budget requests, if you look at the facility master plan, it changes from year to year. No one should site a facility on a plot of land and assume utilities will be there; but, that is how it is typically done. Those supporting the facility don't want the price of the utility systems tacked onto their project, and the institution doesn't want to spend money on utility projects when it needs buildings. One has to ask: "If the system is so messed up, why not change it?" Unfortunately, even with the best intentions, change will simply modify the edges. As long as the process remains in the public sector we will revisit the same problems over and over again. Balancing is required; we need to accept the reality that different priorities and objectives will create constant conflict. Is this approach in fact rational?

I return to the employee survey designed to clarify employee expectations in an effort to improve morale and enhance communication between and among the various levels of the organization's hierarchy. As I noted earlier the survey suggests that employees don't trust management. They feel that the "rules" aren't applied fairly, and that the "system" is not looking out for their interests. "Do you think your work life is getting better, getting worse or staying about the same" was one of the questions posed and responses such as the following were common:

- Getting worse, buildings are being built, renovations are being made but plans for this work are not thought out. Time and time again, major problems arise in a new building because of improper design and planning. So what, let's spend more money and forget about it; it's only money and no one's held responsible.

- Getting worse because of things that are out of our control. Because of the uncertainty in the domestic markets and job cuts everywhere, there is an increased amount of anxiety everywhere.

- Getting worse, no money, but more work.

- Getting worse. Is upper management trying to scare people by saying contract work is cheaper than having in-house workers? Everyone is looking to get the other guy in order to keep the spotlight off of themselves.

- Management constantly lies and uses and abuses workers for its own gain.

When employees were asked about a wish list, what should we or "Management" do to improve your specific job or work life, the responses were varied but several responses seemed universal.

- Give people a raise! Three percent after ten years doesn't cover parking.

- Get rid of some of these managers and supervisors who got where they are because of who they know.

- Upgrade my position. The pay scale for my position is insane. My position is the only job that requires a license, yet we get paid less than or the same as many other jobs.

- A raise would be nice, not just a raise in pay, but a raise in position.

What are the employees telling us? These are serious issues but then they are not new. Survey after survey says the same thing. This survey was taken in 1998; a survey in 2010 said the same thing.

On the other end of the balance bar, the customer wants the lights to work, the heating and cooling system to work, and for us to do "our" job. Their world is being driven by politics, by the budget, by moving forward with strategic planning, business process re-engineering, and continuous improvement. They want the one in the middle to make sure the organization is more efficient. They, along with my bosses, want me to reduce costs and find better (i.e., less expensive) ways of doing business. Everyone wants me to allocate money wisely, to explore contracting out activities when the economics dictate, and to invest in technology to reduce overhead. From their perspective all that seems right, seems reasonable, seems necessary. Yet on the other side, those who work for me see these initiatives as threatening, as efforts to eliminate staff, as the possible loss of their jobs. It would appear that there is more at work here than my perspective. I am walking between two worlds and those worlds see my travel from a different vantage point -- they expect different paths to be taken.

As I participate in a business process review of our "service delivery," I am told to challenge all the non-value-added steps, the steps that do not support the needs of the "end users." Our goal is to streamline the process, to find ways to empower the employee, to question why we do things, to think "out of the box." We use every buzz word ever conceived and we make the process more user-friendly, more streamlined. Unfortunately, when we add back the mandated approval process, when we try to meet the needs of the external customers who provide the funds, when we look at the process from a regulatory perspective, when we consider the need of those who want-who demand – a say in how we use our resources, the new process begins to look very much like the one we threw out, the one that did not meet the customer's needs because it was too time-consuming, too expensive, and too cumbersome. To further complicate my life, the other players (the regulators, the legislators, the private sector, the alumni, my supervisors, and numerous others) all have their agendas.

As I view these agendas I find, once again, that we do not have common objectives. While we may all agree on the global pronouncements of improving service, being more customer-oriented, it doesn't appear we agree on what those goals mean, let alone agree on how to achieve them. Some of the biggest complaints of my customers deal with construction and, not unexpectedly, the age-old issue of initial cost versus maintenance cost. I've alluded to the conflicting priorities within the world of minor renovations but the politics of new construction are even worse and the conflicting priorities go beyond the users and the engineers. As the builders and operators compete, as we strive for different goals, the customer' frustrations grow, for they can't see, they don't expect to see, a difference between those who are responsible for building the building and the ones who maintain it. The customer groups us together and the question is asked over and over again: "Can't you engineers get your act together?" Unfortunately, the answer is no. Why can't we work together and why do I hear from my customers the following complaints: "Why can't we get a building that works? After we move in we get the run around. We call the construction management team and they say call Physical Plant. We call Physical Plant and you say it is the contractor's problem." "We are told the building will be ready and that day comes and goes. Why can't the contractor be held responsible?" "We talk to the construction contractor and he says it is a design problem. The designer says it's a construction problem. Why doesn't someone take responsibility?"

The latest management philosophy to deal with this inevitable conflict is partnering--a coming together of the designer, contractor, user, maintainer, and everyone else who has a part to play in the process "in order to build a commitment to working together in order to shift attitudes, to focus energy and resources away from a defensive posture toward cooperation, shared responsibility, and reduce risk. Partnering offers greater ability to identify problems and concerns early, increases the probability of innovative solutions, and coordinates each phase of the project with greater cooperation among stockholders" (excerpt from a partnering session handout). As with so many of the models, techniques, programs that profess to be the way out of these conflicts I find example after example of declared success. One (Hellmann, 1995) gave the process an A-but reminded everyone that partnering is a process and to make it work everyone must:

- Improve communications.

- Agree on shared goals and objectives.

- Learn to work together.

The author proceeds to list four things that were working well (including communications) and five things (including communicating) that weren't, yet an A-. I don't understand. Partners share, partners understand, partners resolve conflicts. Maintainers and builders are not partners. Haggans (1995) a facilities manager and a practicing architect, suggests that the differences in expectations can trigger a cascade of additional difficulties, lead to the breakdown of communication, and to the development of an adversarial relationship. He states that the architect wants clear direction, instantaneous decisions, tightly designed scope, comfortable budgets, and profitable fees. Meanwhile, the facility manager wants meeting timelines, perfect construction documents, spacious maintenance space, and maintainability built in. At the same time, the university's president wants to dedicate the building on homecoming, the department chair complains the delays will jeopardize research grants, a new professor complains that the room he is getting doesn't meet his needs (the design which is five years old doesn't support a program and equipment that came into being two months ago), and all agree the cost is too high. Yes, increased communication helps but will not solve the problems. The customers are livid – "you engineers are incompetent, you aren't meeting our needs."

The complaints continue; the balancing becomes even more difficult. There are so many team members that we forget who is on the team or what goal we are heading toward. While I appreciate their perspectives, their needs do not coincide with those of others. During the course of an audit, designed to determine how well I'm doing my job, the different perspectives, the different frames of reference become obvious. The auditor needed facts, figures, and quantification, for how else could he determine if I was doing my job? But what was my job from his perspective? If I tell a customer that I can fix his problem but my solution is not the most cost-effective, am I measuring the right thing? Who, what, how do I determine my success? Even worse, if that success calls into question my own values, what do I do? I still want to solve the problem on the surface. Damn the torpedoes, full speed ahead! I know best. It's easy for an inspector to have the answers but he/she doesn't have to implement them, or live with the consequences. This isn't going to be a very congenial relationship.

"People forget how fast you did a job – but they remember how well you did it." Not sure about this one; our customers seem to remember both.

I recall the two biggest lies in the business world. The first -- the inspector tells you he is here to help, and the second is your reply: we are glad you're here! The auditor was a professional; he told me about his past jobs working in facility maintenance, but his perspective was focused on accountability. He asked: "How do you know how productive your people are?" "How do you track material?" "Why aren't your supervisors checking and approving all costs? What is this shop stock (common material in the shop, i.e., nails, screws, wire)?" "How is it accounted for?" We spent hours discussing the importance of accountability and the need to account for every hour of the day. He had a lot of ammunition that supported his position. We had just discovered two employees who had been taking copper from the warehouse and charging it to work orders that obviously didn't require copper. But even with that fact staring at me I argue that too much control thwarts our ability to do our job. I asked, "What about the need for flexibility, the cost of all this control, the need for empowerment, etc., but my arguments didn't carry as much weight as that one piece of paper that couldn't account for the copper. Of course, even the advocates for flexibility would say controls have to be in place. The Federal Express example has become an icon for doing it right -- they know where every package, where every deliveryman is, every minute. Well, maybe not--just a few short weeks before this incident I was complaining to our local utility that a repair team was not on site. I was told by the dispatcher that "the computer" still had them on site; that they hadn't logged out of the area. I told him the service truck had gone through the gate fifteen minutes ago. It is great when others are in the same boat. But perhaps symbolic success is all that is important. If someone thinks you are good, maybe you are.

In theory I like what the auditor described. It would be great to track every minute, every part to an individual task. "Think of the management information you can have," says a consultant. You can do facility costing; you can get a report that tells you which building is costing you the most, information that will help you make better decisions. You can track productivity; the technicians will get more work done. My auditor shares with me information he received over the Internet; like minds sharing good ideas. He tells me of a college that has changed the work order desk to an automated system that automatically takes requests for service. He describes the process as: "We went to a computerized work order system that only needed one clerical person to run it. You call the work orders in on the phone which was answered by the system, although most of the time a human being calls you back for more information. In these days of outsourcing, I'm surprised your physical plant director isn't taking the initiative to be more efficient." Am I missing something here? She actually said, "Most of the time a human being calls you back." What is the measure of this efficiency? Have we really saved any money or just changed methods? How many people did the work before? How many computer programmers did they hire? What were the service call people doing before? What are they doing now? Who calls back? How much did this system cost to install?

As the auditor shared more e-mail, another auditor related their solution to our lack of accountability. "We started to put all (their emphasis) work on work orders and the automated system provided information, information we had to get from individual supervisors before." The author of this solution editorialized about the "sloppiness of the old system." I hope the author was being overly dramatic as he asked: "What if the supervisors left, what if they all contracted Alzheimer's, what if they were the crooks? How would you track costs?" He added: "unless you have a work order to accumulate material and labor for each project there is no way you can have reasonable assurances that the charges are valid or that the University gets value for the payment." Then the knife -- he states: "as you might gather I get resistance when I recommended this in the name of efficiency, in fact one plant manager told me he didn't get paid to be efficient." Well, I offer resistance also but not for that reason. What a complex issue. It sounds easy--the auditor tells me he accounts for hours against projects and many engineering firms do likewise; it is no doubt a great system for allocating time, for sending out bills, but don't tell me it will guarantee productivity. As we talked about the conflicting priorities, I wonder if we were being productive. Were we even working? Why are we doing this? Is the work order system giving us the information we need or is it providing data that we can claim as information? What does it mean if I spend two hours solving one problem and two minutes solving another? Which is a better measure of my productivity? It would be nice to know which building is the most expensive to maintain. Perhaps the answer is an elaborate accounting system, one costing millions to maintain but one that obviously has an air of sophistication, of accuracy. Or perhaps I could simply ask one of the technicians.

Is it me? Am I too thin skinned? At least I'm not alone. With barbs, broadsides and a parody of the bookkeeper's mentality, a state hospital answered an audit of its operation by the State comptroller by issuing a pseudo-scientific report entitled, "Audit of an Audit" (McFadden, 1976). The authors of the rebuttal began their conclusions: "There is no more validity in employing an auditor to evaluate the programs of a hospital than there would be in employing a physician to audit the financial affairs of a bank. Virtually, every recommendation of the auditors, each suggested solution to a problem, each answer to a question, calls directly or indirectly for still more forms, still more paperwork." I appreciate the response may be as biased as the report but I admit I agree with the sentiment. I wasn't a good inspector because I could never look from the outside in. I was always on the inside, asking myself, could I do any better? As one looks at the conflicting goals and objectives influencing our world several terms keep entering the conversation, equal, fair, same, consistency. Fair treatment, equal treatment, are they the same?

Fair, Equal, Same

Everyone wants certainty, wants a rational decision, one that can be duplicated, and one that is the same for everyone. Consistency, certainty, clear guidance, simplicity, quantification - - all terms that imply fairness. Is it too much to ask for clear direction, a focus, consistency, an engineering solution that can be backed up by facts, by figures? I can tell you what the book says, but making the decision is not that easy. Each case is different; each person is different; each set of circumstances is different. It is easy to sit on the sidelines and expect me to give an answer that satisfies everyone. But if I use judgment, everyone will question it. If I strictly follow the rules, I am the very essence of the bureaucrat I dislike. When an employee believes, sincerely believes, he is working hard and therefore deserves a raise - - for doing his job - - how do I give him the answer he wants? When, from an individual's perspective, the answer is obvious, how do I convince him to accept the complexities? People want certainty, but there isn't any. The desire for clear-cut decisions is universal, but in reality few decisions can be clear-cut.

Throughout my journey, my desire to find the answer that satisfied everyone, that met everyone's criteria, that avoided conflict, that solved the problem without creating another has consumed me. My make-up, my education, my being drive me to find a rational decision but I'm seldom successful. My mathematical model, my cost/benefit analysis, my hope to deal with the facts, just the facts, doesn't work very often. The inspector general reports, the auditors, the consultants keep telling me how to solve the problems, but I know the answers are too glib; they sound good but they don't represent reality. Reality is more complex. Reality is listening to the customer complaints, listening to the employees who want more money, juggling priorities, dealing with the employee who is goofing off, and being sensitive to your boss's priorities. Reality is not enough resources, second guessing, political decisions, and emphasizing one side of the coin today and another side tomorrow. I've discovered that my definition of rationality was wrong. I reflect on the perspective of one of my professors, who argues that the only decision that makes any sense is one that takes all the qualifiers into consideration, the one that doesn't focus on just the structural frame, the one that realizes there will be limited information, limited resources, and political realities (Schmidtlein, 1991). I find that being rational has many meanings. There is rational decision-making, the rational actor model described by Allison (1971). This model, my scientific method, relies on clear goals and objectives, alternatives, what consequences rank highest in the decision-makers payoff function. That is how some define a rational view of how the world should act. However, there is a view of rationality that suggests that as long as you accept the underlying premise, the underlying limitations, the ultimate outcome is in fact rational. As you try to make sense of your world it is important for you to understand the various meanings. That understanding will seldom impact success or failure but it will always affect your ability to remain balanced.

Unfortunately, getting those on the ends of the balancing bar to understand these definitions of reality is not easy; I'm not sure it's even possible. As I explain the political decisions to the engineers, they simply do not buy them. That decision is short-sighted; it will cost more money in the long run; it is not the correct engineering solution -- it doesn't make sense from their perspective. Meanwhile, the professor argues that the institution is here to support him/her, that their research pays its fair share and he/she should get good facility support. How do you argue with either perspective? They both can and do offer "rational" arguments. Their needs are real; how do you say no? Will saying no, will saying you have to wait years before we can solve your problem, satisfy anyone? When a customer asks me to solve his/her problem, do we really believe he will acknowledge that his problem is not "big" enough to take high priority -- I've never seen it. Rationality is truly how you define it.

So many of my conversations ultimately lead to the same place, hours are spent on describing how it should be, on the importance of communicating, on how to ensure fairness, on the importance of a long-term perspective, but the immediate problem dictates the response. I understand the emphasis. I agree in principle. I know we need someone to point the herd in the right direction, but for that vision to be successful you need people riding the flanks, eating the dust, chasing the lone calf that breaks loose. I gained great respect for the Air Force's Chief Facility Engineer, and I ended up working for him in a number of capacities over the years. He spent hours discussing his vision. He kept the long-term in perspective, but he was successful because he surrounded himself with a staff that worried about the details, who would spend 12-16 hour days translating the vision to day-to-day action. I was one of the ones dealing with the "day-to-day." I am not the visionary; I am the one in the trenches. While there are examples of where a long-term strategy shaped a short-term decision, when there has to be a choice the short-term perspective typically prevails.

> "Some men dream of worthy accomplishments.
> While other stay awake and do them."

The perils of this perspective, this focus, are often addressed but seldom acted upon and those in the maintenance world can point to example after example of the results of this focus. Titles such as The Decaying American Campus: A Ticking Time Bomb (Rush & Johnson, 1989), and an often quoted line from Hoffer (1969) sums up our frustration: "Any society can be galvanized for a while to build something, but the will and skill to keep things in good repair day in, and day out, are fairly rare." While the significance of Hoffer's work should be viewed in a much wider frame, his assessment of our sustaining power is well stated. If you judge us on our capacity for maintenance, an excellent measure of the vigor and stamina of a society according to Hoffer, we are not doing very well. While the maintainer can point with a knowing look and perhaps some disdain at this acknowledgment, it will do little good to sit back and say "I told you so" as we watch the collapse of the institution's infrastructure. Being right isn't necessarily the best posture if you're the one who has the responsibility for making the equipment work. Strategies, goals, objectives, a long-term perspective point the way, but will we ever get there? Satisfying immediate needs determines our success, and my ability to meet a person's expectations depends upon his or her perspective.

The work of Bolman and Deal (1984) and Kuhn (1962) will confront you at every turn. When structure answers are given to structure problems, everything seems to work well. No one disagrees with applying a formula to determine the economic reorder point for nails in the bin. In that case, we accept quantification, efficiency, a cost/benefits analysis. Unfortunately even this "simple" problem can have its "complex" answers. I will never forget the days of IBM cards (punch cards). As a worker complained to me about a lack of supplies I went to the warehouse and looked in the bin. Perched neatly was a punch card that "represented" the ordered part. The warehouse foreman was fine with it, he had done his job, the part was ordered when it was supposed to be; the card confirmed it. To this day I am certain he wonders what the big deal was, I only wish the piece of production equipment would have been fixed by that piece of card board. When structural or human relations solutions are proposed for political or symbolic problems, or when political or symbolic responses are given when everyone is looking for a structural answer, conflicts begin to grow. Kuhn's (1962) discussion of paradigms, his frame of reference, and his discourse on shared values and commitments help frame my understanding of these complexities. Unfortunately, his work also points out the difficulty a group, a society, will have dealing with them. But, these complexities must be understood because they cause a tremendous amount of conflict and mistrust. The engineers, the technicians, asked over and over again, "Why aren't you supporting us?" "We need more people to get the job done. Our salaries are below market. You want, you expect us to do more but we aren't recognized for what we do." "The roof needs to be replaced now. Can't you see how much it is costing us to patch it every time it rains? Why can't you fund its replacement?" "Don't tell me there are other priorities; this is costing a lot of money." Yes, but it's from a different pot of money. How do I explain that to someone who doesn't understand the politics of the budget? I have trouble accepting it and I do understand. Similarly, we attempt to sell reorganizations as the answer to the problems of public sector financing, but the political realities thwart any organizational structure. Surely we don't expect an organization to give up the opportunity to open a new building because the maintainers are concerned about the long-term consequences of such action. No one is going to tell the base commander we can't meet his priorities because our rules say we can't do it.

A truckload of 2 by 4s is but one reminder of "the different frames of reference." I recall the following with great clarity even though it happened many years ago. A maintenance organization on base was building a wall out of scrap lumber. They were literally nailing foot-long pieces of 2 by 4s together to make an eight-foot stud. When I asked why, they responded "The engineers [my staff] said there weren't any 2 by 4s in the warehouse." This was true, in one sense; I also knew we had another warehouse full of lumber against our war readiness stock. The rules said this had to be available (in case of war); it was a separate account and the warehouse staff knew they weren't to use it. The rules were clear; if we had an inspection and we were short a few "war-ready 2 by 4's" I would be written up. The inspectors would be doing their job, and from their perspective, the rules, the structural frame of reference, made it right. The system was in equilibrium, but I just couldn't live with it. I got them the lumber; if we went to war, I'd get it back. It made sense to me, but it upset the system. The conflict was not an exception; there are so many examples. The political frame of reference says we must measure performance. Symbolically it makes sense; structurally we can develop a system, but can structural programs change the human's perspective? How do you ensure that the number of outstanding employees is the five percent that the bell-shaped curve suggests? One has to select a number; it is the only way. You force the system to predetermine how many people are outstanding. Five percent makes sense from a quantitative perspective. The budget community likes it from a structural perspective (we know how much money is needed). Politically it is an acceptable number, but, from a human perspective, it doesn't work. How do you tell people that only five percent that can be selected and that the selection process will be objective? We will "back" into the right number and the process will be subjective. There is no other way. Will the employees see it as fair? Not if they weren't selected, not if someone they believed shouldn't get it was selected, not if they realized that I just "know" who my best performers are because they get the job done. I know who does and who doesn't work well with others, but will everyone agree? If I look at it from someone else's perspective, what will I see?

I recall vividly a fairly young sergeant who would do anything I asked. An expert equipment operator, he could make a 20-ton snow plow perform magic. He would work for hours and I would have to force him off the truck. If I had three more like him I could do without ten others. As a commander I had the ability to promote him on the spot and I planned to do so; no one from my perspective deserved it more. As I moved forward, a crusty old sergeant told me not to do it, others would not be supportive. I couldn't believe it. How could anyone see it differently? He then informed me the young man had a drinking problem and when he "fell off the wagon" they would hide him from me. Don't be quick to condemn anyone. If the chips were down, I'd still count on him, but I couldn't promote him. As I dealt with the situation, there was no way to win. The human relations frame was pleased (I got him help). The structural frame was unhappy (productivity suffered when I took him off the crew), the political frame was oblivious (thank goodness there hadn't been an accident), and those in the symbolic frame were confused (those who saw him as a hard worker didn't understand why he wasn't promoted; others wanted to know why I didn't demote him). I was powerless. I wasn't going to be able to satisfy everyone.

I return to the work of Bilello (1993) and his use of different frames of reference to view the very concrete process of building but a building is not the end product. A building is a process and there is no one right way to build. The process must be viewed from many directions. The engineer must look through the eyes of the architect; the architect looks through the eyes of the customer. My dream is that all start to look through the eyes of the maintainer. But as we see this shared vision the process becomes very complicated. As we give up our view, we give up some of our control. That is an uncomfortable position. That is the most perplexing reality, because we tend to give up responsibility as we give up control. If it is not mine to control, therefore it is not mine to be responsible for.

What does it mean if the employees do or don't trust me? Do those who work for me have confidence in me? What do they want me to do? How am I to help them? Do they want or need my protection? What comfort can I provide? Does trust imply loyalty? Trust has become one of the watchwords for leaders, for leadership in the 1990's. Fairholm (1994) argues that the lack of trust is crippling more and more organizations in today's highly competitive environment. So how do I become trustworthy? The employees want me to defend them, to protect them from those who would challenge them, question them or threaten them. My predecessor would take on any challenger, would defend the employees against all complaints, but he created an us-versus-them environment. Are you loyal to your employees if you take up their case? But how do you do that if you are supposed to move beyond your organization to become a team player? We expect everyone to subordinate his or her personal goals to those of the team, and to do so because the organization is structured so that everyone shares in the team result (Fairholm, 1994). But are organizations so structured? Trust is supposed to be the result of people seeing themselves united in common pursuits and seeing that their associates have the desire and know-how to pursue goals in a mutually compatible way. At least that is the argument. However, even those who suggest this is the way it should be admit that while the emphasis should be on shared objectives and shared values, organizations do not exist independent of the subjective interest of those who comprise them (Fairholm, 1994). It sounds like a Catch 22 again. Benveniste (1989) suggests that something is radically wrong with the mindset that is being used at work, and that people are using an overly rational approach that implies more logic and objectivity than what actually exists. He concludes that before trusting relationships are possible, one first has to recognize that political forces, which create mistrust, are inherent in any situation and that we must deal skillfully with them. To have trust we have to accept an environment in which a lack of trust is likely (Culbert & McDonough, 1985). This is going to be a pretty difficult path to follow.

To make matters worse, trust will be jeopardized when some in an organization withholds trust because of a failure of others to provide proof of their support (Fairholm, 1994). I think back to the surveys, to my conversation with my employees, they don't trust management. I can't give them the answers they want. I can't prove to them I am supporting their objectives (especially if I have to yield to the objectives of the bigger team). I shouldn't be surprised at the results. Trust is a quality that people extend to those who appear to offer them support and who value their contributions to the organization's effectiveness (Culbert & McDonough, 1985). I'm in trouble, for those who argue that leadership can't take place in a culture in which people aren't members of the "bigger team," who doubt others' motives or sincere intent, or pursue independent agendas, are describing my world. Why can't we place our interests below those of the whole team? It is not because people aren't trying. It is not because people don't see themselves as contributing, but the various structures, the various groups, the conflicting goals and agendas prevent them from seeing the big picture, let alone supporting it. Organizations, like people, do not always act in the way our theories, or even common sense, would suggest (Berkley, 1984). Culbert and McDonough (1985) suggest that trust depends upon agreed upon expectations, a supportive environment, and a respect for individual differences. How can we disagree with that? Who wouldn't want to be in an organization based on those principles? However, Harvey (1989) suggests that distrust is bred by ambiguity, subjectivity, and that organizations and decisions made by them, that aren't supported by objectivity, will be considered untrustworthy.

I find myself on the tightrope again. We stress productivity and I'm accused of more work for no additional pay. Economically-sound decisions, decisions that are supported by analysis, by engineering calculations, are changed because of political issues. Employees see money going for new buildings, but we tell them there is no money for raises. Part of me accepts the conflicts, but part of me condemns the policies. Part of me wants to escape from the need to subjugate the needs, the desires, of those who work for me for the common good of the organization; but part of me realizes that the system will, and must, prevail. Part of me wants to tell the employees to just go to work; but part of me want to tell my bosses that they don't understand what goes on in the trenches.

There is no way in our world can expect, demand fair, equal, same. Can equal and fair co-exist? If I give an "office worker" a fifteen minute break, can I give the worker who just came out of a utility vault, that was at 110 degrees, a twenty minute break? Is that equal? No. Is it fair? Absolutely. Should I give an employee who is never late the same discipline I give to the employee who is "always" late? "Of course not" is the answer, but I'm told I must be consistent. How do you rate one member of a work crew differently than another? We stress teamwork, we stress working together, yet we evaluate individually. What distinguishes an "exceeds expectations" when the criteria is "foster teamwork?" I can do it based on my judgment, my observation, but don't tell me to quantify it. The performance evaluation tracking film shows me how to count errors for a telephone operator. That makes sense, I can quantify that; too bad there aren't any more telephone operators. Try defining what is clean for a custodial worker, we all know it when we see it, but when the chips are down we won't agree how to measure it.

Same, fair, trust, consistency, equal... the words rolling out of every consultant's mouth and are claimed to be the answer to every management and personnel problem. But I'm sorry, the world is not fair, trust usually means "support me and give me what I want," and the faculty has their set of rules the staff has another. The "workforce" who punches time clocks are not treated the same as the "office worker" who can work from home. The inconsistencies are everywhere and none more complex than customer service.

Customer Service vs. Customer Servant

"If we don't take care of the customer, someone else will." The poster stares at me. So our job isn't about fixing pipes or producing steam. It is about customer comfort; it is about measuring our ability to meet the customer's expectations. We are told they expect efficiency, effectiveness, productivity, quantification, rational decisions, cost/benefit analysis and they want to be able to compare us to others who can do our job, so they can obtain the best (i.e., least expensive) service, but to make the comparison you need numbers, scales, criteria. We have to be able to justify our existence. Have we become so committed to providing customer service that we neglect the server? Roger Dow (1997), vice president of Marriott, offers this glimpse into the world of the server:

> A traveler was holding up the line at the Delta Airlines counter in Chicago, screaming at the woman at the counter. His bags had been misplaced or rerouted. His face is all red, he's yelling at her, he's calling her an idiot, he's saying he's never going to fly

Delta airlines as long as he lives, he's going to tell every person he knows, and when the word gets out (because people listen to him), no one will fly their airline, and they're going to go bankrupt. All of a sudden she stopped his tirade and said, "Sir, you're getting all excited. Do you understand that there are only two people who care if you ever get your bags back? And one of us is losing interest real fast."

I don't know if it is a true story or just an amusing anecdote, but we need to pay heed to what it says. Unfortunately the rest of the story probably goes like this: the customer complains to, or writes a letter to, the employee's supervisor who in turn chastises the employee and says, "Those of us in the service industry have to understand that the customer is always right and we are here to meet his needs; it doesn't matter what the customer says, you have to smile and 'create' a positive experience." The examples of customer service, good and bad, are everywhere.

One of the first official requests made by a new department head in our local hospital was directed to the maintenance department for the repair of a leak under one of the sinks. Promptly, a maintenance employee appeared with a bucket which he positioned under the drip. He assured her that, when other more urgent requests had been satisfied, a plumber would be assigned to make the necessary repairs. For the present, however, would she appoint someone to empty the bucket periodically? One of her last official acts, before retiring after 15 years of service, was to report that the pail which had served so faithfully had sprung a leak. Shortly, a maintenance man arrived -- with a shiny new bucket (Reader's Digest).

I discovered this article in 1975 and used it to introduce my lectures on customer service. I found it to be a cute story and it was usually good for a laugh or at least a chuckle. I would conclude my remarks by telling the facility engineers not to leave any buckets. As I finished a lecture at a national conference of hospital administrators, a participant came forward to tell me she was the new department head and that the bucket was still there. I found it a little unbelievable but also a little comforting. I thought I was the only one who had left buckets.

As I search the literature and talk to others, I find example after example of the same frustrations, but nothing is said about the experience of dealing with the issues. Yes, there are many who can tell me what is wrong; yes, there are many who say they have an answer; but there are few, if any, who deal with the reality of being the one in the middle. A <u>Washington Post</u> headline screams: "District Faces Avalanche of Problems Maintaining a Crumbling Infrastructure" (Jan. 29, 1996, A-8). Pat Choate, an often-quoted authority on the decaying public infrastructure, concludes: "The consequences of not dealing with problems until you have a storm are not obvious. Governments can get away with it politically. You can pull back money on repairs and maintenance; however, at some point the game catches up to you." But when it catches up who is holding the ball? The article continues: "Cities and counties will always be playing catch up. Preventive maintenance is a constant concern and to be honest about it, there is never enough money to do it right. Preventive maintenance does not have a constituency out there lobbying for it. "It's invisible, out of sight, out of mind." As for the District, Choate says: "the facility engineer has a monster job on his hands." For most, the monster goes into hiding once the current crisis is handled; however, for the engineer, the monster is always just outside the door.

Yet once the monster is out, everyone has a solution. When a seven-year-old student flushed a public school toilet, causing it to spew scalding water that scarred her for life, the state inspector had the answer: "State Faults Schools on Boiler Safety" reads the headlines (Baltimore Sun, Sept. 15, 1996). The article describes a series of system failures, a lack of a sense of urgency, and poor maintenance procedures. All of a sudden there is finger pointing, there are promises to make sure the engineer is doing preventive maintenance and inspecting. What an easy answer. Don't they think we know what to do? Why wasn't it done before? Is it incompetence, as so many suggest? It is easy to be a Monday morning quarterback. It is easy to say how it should have been done, but the easy answer in no way describes the agony of the one who knows how it should be done but who also knows that if he/she were in the same boat it would still happen. I have been there. As a consultant, I told a base level engineer that he had to develop a work plan and identify the requirements. Then, and only then, would the headquarters be able to fund his needs. The base had the worst facilities in England. Everyone could see the requirements; the need for additional maintenance funds was obvious. However, the system required, demanded, justification. An in-service work plan that identified the work to be done and the resources that were needed to do it was the only way to garner those resources, I told him. Unfortunately, since the base hadn't done that, additional funding wouldn't be forthcoming. As luck, or fate, would have it, I became that base level engineer. I had access to the report that I, in another life, had written. I spent the next several months developing the plan. I spent literally hundreds of hours after the normal duty day defining the requirements, developing the plan, justifying the obvious need for additional resources. I packaged it, forwarded it to the headquarters, and waited for the additional, badly needed resources. Unfortunately, none were forthcoming. Their response? The typical, expected response: "You must prioritize the requirements; your most pressing requirements should be funded within the existing funding levels." I had to laugh; the answer was expected; it made sense; it was the only response that could have been given, but it wasn't as advertised. Different perspectives, different objectives--the headquarters couldn't funnel "extra" resources to one base; what would the others say?

In 1995, the University of Massachusetts called in a team of experts to develop a plan designed to "make the campus maintenance department more efficient today," while plans to "find $660 million needed to repair years of neglect" were developed (Springfield Union, Feb. 10, 1995, p. 20). An interesting choice of words: Plan to compensate for a $660 million shortfall, representing years of reduced funding, by making the current organization more efficient. This is a pretty tall order. The report concluded the campus needs $33 million a year for over the next 20 years, that the campus was being strangled by state regulations that add time and money to campus priorities, and that the in-house staff was badly organized and ineffective. Unfortunately, all the emphasis was placed on the last problem, the one that was easiest to attack, but the one with the least impact on the real problems.

The problems are universal (Rush & Johnson, 1989). The report could have been written at virtually any college or city that you can name, and the answers can be predicted without reading the report. I know the answers; I wrote the answers in another lifetime. The answers, at best, will result in some additional resources, a few changes in priority, but they will not change the process. The first answer to the problem was to reorganize and increase communications, to enact a continuous improvement program, to reduce the layers of management, and to become more customer oriented. The second answer was to develop a mission statement, and then the classic answer was given: "conduct facility audits to identify repair requirements and earmark 1.5 to 2.5 percent of the plant replacement value to solve the deferred maintenance problems" (Kaiser, 1993). I wonder if the experts really believed that the existing managers had not thought of those ideas? The solutions sound so easy. Of course, other experts got on the bandwagon as the word got around. The state legislators stressed accountability, condemned the poor organization of the physical plant, and wanted to know why the state hadn't held the architects and contractors accountable for poorly designed and constructed building. Wait a minute, the legislators are the state! Their rules, regulations, and policies lead to the structure that "allows" this to happen. It is so easy to tell people what to do. Ultimately the Director of the Physical Plant was reassigned and a search for a new one began -- a search to find a person who could change the culture.

Why does it take a crisis to identify the issues? I don't have to do facility inspections; give me the $600 million and I'll fix the years of neglect. The consultants may have legitimized the process but their insight won't solve the problem. But then maybe the process is the solution. A crisis focuses attention; attention causes people to channel their efforts; channeling efforts and an influx of resources can lead to change. Maybe the whole thing is the way it has to be; how depressing. In their book, <u>A Passion for Excellence</u>, Peters and Austin (1985) recognize the Air Force's Tactical Air Command for turning their facilities around with <u>no</u> increase in budget. That simply is not true. While the operations and maintenance budget remained the same, the pie was certainly divided up differently. There is no question that management's attention was focused on the deteriorating facilities and that the correction of long-standing problems was made a priority, but fixing the problem required increased resources. Even at that, much of the money was spent on exterior cosmetics, i.e., painting, landscaping, furnishings, and the building systems (heating, cooling, electrical, etc.) continued to deteriorate. Yet success was declared.

Who can argue with those who want us to improve service? However, I have no respect for those who sit on the sidelines and tell me I can compensate for a $600 million short fall by reorganizing. We built facilities on the old airfield in Sicily because we did not have a choice, not because we didn't know any better. We failed to fix the boiler because of conflicting priorities, not because we were incompetent. We cut the grass instead of repairing roofs because both are important, not because we consider cutting grass more important than roofs. But then, can new blood change the perspective of the organization? While I say we never change, change occurs all the time. But are we simply shifting emphasis? In my experience, reorganizing doesn't typically solve the underlying problems. A new wiring diagram may move an obstacle out of the way for a while, but the obstacle remains. What does the customer really want? From my vantage point the following expose says it all.

> In most groups, if you say the words "maintenance person" people form a mental picture in their minds: a person in an oil-spotted work shirt with buttons straining to hold together fabric stretched tight over a belly too large to stuff inside a belt which itself is straining to hold up a massive ring of keys. Some would say "a necessary evil." An unpleasant cost of doing business. Whereabouts: nowhere to be found or in the break room. Question: What is white, has wheels and sleeps four? Answer: A Physical Plant van (obviously a well-used refrain, many versions but the sentiment is the same). Most people have no idea what maintenance people do in a large and diverse physical plant organization. They are not around at night to see the response made to an emergency, or on the roof in a downpour to observe the unclogging of a drain, or in a mechanical equipment room where operational adjustments require a real pro. They never see the effort made

to restore failed electrical power, or midnight irrigation shifts, or the emergency repairs made to a leaking boiler or chilled water coil, or the scramble necessary to replace a failed compressor. But let the temperature rise a few degrees, or a waste basket not get emptied, or have a flickering light, and a crisis is in the offering. And when the maintenance worker takes a break, everyone assumes he or she is just goofing off. When everything is working, the temperature is within acceptable limits, the buildings are clean, and the grounds are litter free, no one notices. But let anything go "off-normal" and there is a crisis to resolve, a letter of explanation to write, and ruffled feathers to smooth. But then, that is the way of life in maintenance. We are at our best when no one notices us. In an ideal world, maintenance workers would be judged strictly upon the quality of their work.
> --Val Peterson, Past President
> Association of Physical Plant
> Administrators

In an ideal world, what a wonderful concept -- too bad there isn't one. As I talk to customers, as I begin to see their view of my world, my dreams of uncomplicated, easily-defined success are shattered. Their perspective is different from mine; they see my world from a unique vantage point; their reality does not correspond with mine.

As I talked to my customers, several phrases were repeated over and over again. Solve my problem. Costs too much, takes too long. Provide better service. Be more productive. Ensure responsiveness. All common refrains, but do we understand each other? Do we agree on the meaning of the words that are used to describe our relationship? Visions of shared goals, of shared objectives, shared expectations fade as I reflect on what it means to provide service. As I try to reconcile their demands for accountability and productivity, I lose faith in my ability to balance the conflicting priorities. Why do our customers see us in the light that Val Peterson exposed? I repeat the guiding principles: the customer is always right, service is our most important product, take care of the customer or someone else will--the slogans are ageless, as are the demands. Solve my problem. Why did it take so long? Why can't you manage the workforce? The phrases roll off my tongue. Unfortunately, I am not any better when I complain when the lights go out at my house, when I can't get a real live person on the line, when the insurance company won't cover a bill. We are all customers.

For me the most visible, the most talked about, some would say the most important, customers are the students, faculty, and staff, and they all require a roof over their heads, proper temperature control, and numerous electrical outlets. But who has the priority? Do I respond to a power outage in a classroom before I get power back to a research lab? The easy answer, the expected answer, is to properly manage my resources to do both. While that is usually the case, let's assume I have to make a choice. Given that scenario, is there an agreed-upon decision-making process? Does the strategic plan place teaching over research? Can I quantify the cost of two hundred students missing an hour lecture and compare it to the cost of a researcher missing one hour of research data? What criteria can I use to determine which one is more important to the mission of higher education? As complex as this world is, it gets worse. Not all of our customers are two-legged. I reflect on the criticism levied on us by a researcher when we didn't get to an animal care facility within five minutes . . . "you can't treat animals the way you treat humans!" was his perspective. Some days you can't win. As I install curb cuts for those in wheelchairs, I receive complaints from those without sight because they can no longer feel the curb line. I install "dimples" on the ramps to provide "the needed feel" only to find that ice, which can't be shoveled, builds up in the crevices. Now I've created a safety hazard for everyone. Sometimes trying to meet the goals of a "simple concept" like customer service gets pretty frustrating. We view the same scene from completely different directions.

A professor, who demanded the locks on his lab be changed after a computer was stolen, now wants cleaning supplies since we no longer clean his lab (because we no longer have keys). He can't understand why the custodian, who can hardly speak English, can't give him what he needs, especially since he now has to do our job. He complains that when his graduate students decided to clean up the lab one afternoon our inability to manage, our inflexibility, our bureaucracy got in his way and wasted the graduate students' time. "Why can't you be flexible?" he asks. I wonder but don't ask, "Why can't you understand that managing several Ph.D. students is not the same as managing 300 custodial workers?" Empowering sounds like a great idea, but so does strict control over easily pilfered cleaning supplies. It is easier, it is more efficient, to have clear-cut guidelines, to limit authority, to "manage by the numbers" than it is to expect an employee to decide when, to whom, and under what circumstances it is permissible to give cleaning supplies away. Don't tell me we need to meet everyone's needs; we've got hundreds of classrooms and restrooms to clean in four hours and we need structure. I want to solve the researcher's problem but it will create others; is this really where you want me to spend my time? He wants flexibility; I need order.

Another professor complained that he had spent a lot of his time, and his department's money, to develop high tech, innovative teaching methods, but that his work was wasted because the university placed him in a lecture hall with a post blocking the view of several students. "The university needs to do something!" was his view. Wait, he is the University -- or is he? Why is he teaching in this lecture hall instead of one of the newer ones on campus? "They are too far away, they belong to another department," is the response. Why can't several sessions of the same class be taught so a smaller, better-equipped room can be used, I wonder? I obviously don't understand, but neither does he. The lecture hall he is complaining about was to be replaced ten years ago and those before us made the decision to "live with them until they are replaced," a wise decision at the time. Of course, the lecture hall is still being used because its replacement has been deferred once again. Good planning was done; it just got replaced by another good plan. The replacement of that classroom isn't the highest priority, but how can that be? I'm being naive, but the professor doesn't care, it's not his problem; he can't teach the way he wants and I can't argue with his perspective. He's right but so am I. Is customer service just another name for customer servant? "One of the most frustrating situations I ever experienced is when one of your mechanics said," "'I'll check on it and get back to you' and then I never hear from him again." The customer goes on. "Often when you engineers arrive to examine a problem you talk among yourselves and then leave. The old 'look and leave syndrome.' No information is shared with us as to whether a part must be ordered or whether the problem is solvable. One is left guessing." Various versions of this complaint are shared by everyone I talk to. And no doubt you have your own. In most cases, people just wanted to have someone tell them what was going on. Reasonable requests to be sure. Fostering customer service is my biggest challenge; we do well at times; at others, we fail miserably. Why is this so hard? Why can't we just decree it to be done? If this is such a big problem, why don't we have the energy to solve it? Re-engineer the process, the consultants say. But that is easier said than done. I can develop a process, I can write it down on paper, and articulate a method that will meet these objectives but then I add in the people, I add in competing objectives, add in the "fog of war" (Clauzwitz, 1976) and the plan seems to unfold.

The lack of customer follow-up continues to be a problem, yet I don't know why we can't, don't just do it. Is it just inconvenient? Are we too busy getting the job done to realize talking to the customer is part of the job? On the other hand, if someone reports a leaking faucet, how much time do I spend trying to find the customer? Am I providing service? Does that mean I am to be a servant? Example after example of poor service was given and the conversations take on a common theme: we want our problems solved. I (we) can solve any of the surface problems individually, but how do you make each problem the one that is given your undivided attention? Each problem has an answer but who balances the requirements? Who is first? Who waits?

Over the years I've had bosses who insisted, not in a joking manner although I took it that way, that we didn't have problems, we had opportunities. Today it seems we seek win-win solutions to problems so there are no winners or losers, just all winners, and in all cases a solution is implied. When I think of problems, I think back to my mathematical frame of reference. I want, I need, a solution--the one right, the one and only solution--the one you get by "plugging" in a value for X to get Y. But that is not the only definition of a problem. The ancient Greeks thought of a problem as a question put forward for discussion. How did a question for discussion become a problem for solution? We have become enamored with solving problems. We are determined to find the one right solution. Yet, in our world, problems don't fit the mathematical model. There are no simple answers, and most problems being dealt with in the workplace are issues (Schmidtlein, 1991). Issues aren't solved, issues are dealt with. Decisions are made, but those decisions are judgments and those judgments are made based on incomplete information and deal with distributing limited resources. Judgment, subjective evaluations, different frames of reference all imply making the "best call." However, this lack of quantification places one at odds with those who disagree with the decisions. It seems that solving one problem gives rise to more problems. There is no one easy answer; the examples are everywhere.

The problem for the customer is not the broken air handler-- his problem is his inability to get his work done. The problem with the air handler is not the broken part -- it is the fact that the unit should have been replaced years ago. But the replacement problem is not that the unit can't be replaced--it is the lack of funds to replace all of them that need replacing. But the customers don't care about all of those (my) problems; they can't do their work because I can't provide the facility support they expect. I've come full circle, the buck stops here. It's nobody's fault that the unit needs to be replaced, but someone has to make the call. Why can't the decision be made lower in the organization? It can't be made lower because the mechanics don't control the funds. Unfortunately, I don't control enough funds but I'm responsible for getting it fixed; more importantly, I should have prevented it from happening. Get a handle on the problem, is the cry of my bosses. Put a system in place that prevents this from happening, suggests the consultant. But it will happen again.

Problems! They may be called opportunities, they may be called issues, they may be called a lot of things, but there is one thing for sure- we want to quantify them and solve them. But there are no answers, for the problems we deal with are "wicked problems." Rittel and Webber (1973) suggest that these wicked problems may never be solved and moreover, there is never a clear cut, self-evident solution that everyone would be willing to accept anyway. Benveniste (1989) notes that most planning or policy problems are complex, goals are often unclear and often vague or confusing. He goes on to say that some will never agree with the goals, and even those who agree with the goals won't agree on the way to reach them. Wicked problems are the curse of many professions.

Lee (1991), a teacher, a researcher, a fellow traveler on this path, shares my frustration as she deals with multiple choice questions. Her students argue that multiple choice questions are objective, that they are either right or wrong, and that the teacher's subjectivity will not enter into the evaluation process. Fair, equitable, and easy all come to mind. But Diane is concerned about this desire for a single truth. Diane wants her students to realize that, to be authentic professionals, they have to reject the notion of fixed value, fixed goals; instead they should be seeking a quest for what it means to be thinker, a teacher in the world of wicked problems. I also long for that revelation, for I must accept the technical, the physical, and the political and economic constraints that translate into the inability to make fair, equitable, easy decisions. Rittel and Webber (1973) suggest what is special about wicked problems is that it is not the solution that matters so much as the process at arriving at an outcome. Churchman (1971) writes about real life and wicked problems as juxtapositions to puzzles--but I want the solution. I'm not cut out for dealing with the process. I want the end. I recall, with some dismay, the little puzzles that contained clown faces under a plastic cover. You had to maneuver, tip and balance the box in order to get the little steel balls to roll into the cutouts that were the clown's eyes and nose. It took time, it took patience, the process was the game but I yanked the top off and set the ball in the right places. I want the problem solved so I can move to the next one.

The service sector has become a major part of American industry during the last several decades and as manufacturing declines and more people are asking how do you measure success in this type of environment? In manufacturing, the process is easy; you simply measure the cost per widget. Everything can be explained by that one simple number. If your product costs more that the competitor's, you know it, but what about the service industry? We start by using catchy phrases, we say: service is our most important product, service with a smile, the customer is always right. But how do you measure those products? What are the costs to produce that service? In some part of the service industry (banks, fast food chains, etc.) you can measure the bottom line--assets held, over 1,000,000 sold, but what is our measure of success in the public sector, especially in facility maintenance? I can do customer surveys; I can keep track of the average time to complete a service call. I can count the backlog, but at what cost do I provide the expected level of service?

As we've moved away from mass production to service and information, there has been a change in emphasis from control of behavior and measurement of outputs to control of employee attitudes and commitments (Alvesson, 1993). But the questions remain: how do I know I've created that commitment and at what cost? Do I have carpenters standing by to respond to every call? Do I meet everyone's timelines? Whose do I meet? Whose do I put behind? I reflect back to an attempt to explain to the customers that our carpenter shop in England did not have as many carpenters as one might expect, having come from a Stateside base. I wanted to educate the customers; I wanted them to understand that our British workers might not be able to respond as expected. Unfortunately, I made a fatal mistake by saying: Our carpentry shop is unlike the one you may have come to know at Stateside bases. We don't have the equipment or staffing to meet every priority. In retrospect I failed to influence the customer; no one called me to say I could delay their jobs. But what I did do was insult the very people I was trying to support. My effort to gain understanding was taken by the carpenters as a slap at their abilities. My article ended up on the center of the shop's dartboard with an uncomplimentary _____, Jack!

Does service mean meeting the customer's every need? Peters (1985) and every consultant I've ever met tells the Nordstrom story of customer service. It seems that a customer expected to have a suit ready as he departed for a business trip but it wasn't. Leaving for the trip, his opinion of Nordstrom sank until he arrives at his hotel to find a Federal Express package (with $98 postage) waiting for him. It contained his suit and three silk ties and an apology from Nordstrom. The story has grown in proportion; it has become the epitome of customer service and it also speaks well of Federal Express. But how often can you take that extra step? After a while, you'll go broke. The story is great, but the auditors, the budget officer, and the company wouldn't let it happen very often. What does one do when providing great service to one means a delay to another? Has service become synonymous with being at the customer's beck and call, being a servant perhaps? What limits do we place on this service? If I'm selling a product, that service may result in another sale. But if I'm providing a service, and the service doesn't cost the customer anything, what exchange mechanism is there to determine the value of the "product?" Raising the customer's expectations is expected, almost encouraged, and our ability to meet those expectations had become a measure of our success. But at what cost? Success for the builder is measure opening--day does the building look nice? The measure of success for the maintainer begins the next day and lasts for a long time. What is holding up that false front?

> "The difference between ordinary and
> extraordinary is that little extra."

The words "customer service" has become synonymous with a measure of our job performance. Service is no longer the task; it is a measure of how well we perform. If we don't meet the customer's demands, we are not providing the service. Yet, no one defines the limits. "Customer service" --it sounds right; symbolically it is what is expected; politically it sells; structurally we can measure it by surveys, by polls, but what is the cost? I need that balance. Daigneau (1997) addresses the problem of the facility maintenance industry when he acknowledges that it is difficult to relate the service aspect of facilities management with production aspect of manufacturing. He notes that after buying a product you own the product, but after receiving a service you own only a memory. He concludes that a defective product can be recalled. Poor service delivery cannot, because only the memory of the experience remains. I agree wholeheartedly and I look for a way to ensure success; not surprisingly, I find many who promise me that service. For example, Daigneau (1997), speaking to facility managers, advocates a process he calls, "Product Based Management." He says it is not another management fad, but "while not a fad" it is a description of the age old process: identify your customer, determine his needs, and meet those needs. I can't finish. It's repackaging again. I know what I'm supposed to do; it's in the doing that I have difficulty. While the customer may always be the customer, that doesn't mean I can always provide the service they expect. These tensions result in more than just conflicts over repairing broken ceiling tile. The customers express feelings of a lack of control, of an inability to influence the people who provide them with the facilities they need to get their jobs done. I am not a part of their world; their world is the job they do, their research, their teaching, the tasks that govern their lives. And, they are not a part of mine. When a light doesn't work, they are not concerned about the why; they are concerned about its inability to meet their needs. More importantly, they don't control the process of getting it fixed. What prevents them from taking action into their own hands? While changing a light bulb may be a trivial issue, and while I can understand their inability to build a new building, I don't understand the lack of desire to influence the process that controls those decisions. On the one hand, the customers are frustrated about not controlling their destiny (from a facilities perspective), but on the other hand, they don't take the steps to enter my world to influence it. It seems that two extremes prevail. On the one hand, a professor argues: I tried to get things fixed but just gave up. "I decided that I would just have to "live" with the poor conditions. I didn't have time to do my work, my research, and try to work through your bureaucracy at the same time. I just don't care anymore. You won't hear from me until your failures affect my work."

This is an interesting perspective. On the other hand, there are those who have found me. I have become their inroad to my world; they have found that a call to me will get results. Their approach is to go outside the system. If the system doesn't respond, I'll find a way around the "normal" process, is their perspective. For their approach to work, I have to manipulate the rules of my system and frustrate those who dutifully wait in line. Am I successful on the surface because I violate the very tenets of the rules that provide order?

Customer service verses customer servant is just one of the difficulties facing any middle manager. Your customer may be external, they may be internal but it doesn't matter. We are expected to find a way, but at the same time "follow the rules." Treat people fairly, i.e., the same, but you better know who you can trust when the chips are down. One soon learns who you can count on; one soon learns who does what needs to be done to meet a customers' or your boss's demands. You are expected to treat that individual the same as the one who always has an excuse, the one who is out the door as quitting time arrives. Don't tell me there is no difference in those people; don't tell me not to give the "good" employee the benefit of the doubt. It all seems to come down to one issue, perceptions verses reality.

Perceptions vs. Reality - What is Real

What if what you believe creates your reality; what if where you sit determines where you stand? What if perspective is everything?

As I talk to one of our "supporters," he relays an all too common complaint. It is a Tuesday and a classroom is hot. A faculty member complains to his chair, the chair call the dean's secretary (she "monitors" the college's work orders) and she calls our work control center. The work control technician (a part-time student employee) writes the work order; it is sent to the shop, assigned to a mechanic, and enters the queue. At first blush, the answer to this "bureaucracy" is to redesign the process so it doesn't take so long. But that's not the answer; the process is not the problem. The secretary tells the work control technician to have the mechanic contact the department that made the complaint and that is where the normal process begins to fall apart. On Thursday, the classroom is still hot because the mechanics who responded to the problem on Wednesday had to order a replacement motor. The mechanic told "someone" that the unit would be up and running Thursday afternoon. Unfortunately, on Thursday morning some other faculty member complained, but this time the chair e-mails the dean, and the dean e-mails me, but not until Friday. By the time I sort through all of the communications, I find that the unit has been repaired and, given the staffing levels, the age of the equipment, the procurement process, other priorities, etc., the process worked pretty well. But I had wasted hours chasing a problem that wasn't a problem. Not from my perspective anyway. But what about the dean's perspective?

> "It would have been helpful if someone had called the chair sooner. [He continues:] I know, I know, there are other emergencies, one needs to wait his turn, there is only so much you can do with the people you have, and it would be nice if people could understand all of this. Unfortunately when you have yelling faculty in your

office telling you that they cannot teach and are beside themselves, it does provoke a strong reaction and a need to act."

I understand and it's nice he understands, but what do I do? That exchange, or ones very similar to it, happen every day and they all provoke strong reactions.

As we conduct a series of meetings to let the customers know about an upcoming renovation project, the engineers have high expectations. The project required some asbestos abatement: a very easy task, but a very emotional subject. All the right explanations are given; all of the controls are in place; the process is safer than walking across the street, but the occupants remain skeptical. An occupant summed it up after a long, long discourse:

"We understand the procedure, we understand that it is safe, <u>rationally</u> it all makes sense <u>but</u> emotions take over and we want to be out of the building [even though they are floors away, in a completely different area] when the work is done." Then add the inevitable: "You take care of it or we'll tell the Dean, the newspapers will find out about it, and we'll call the EPA."

Go ahead and complain, is my first reaction; you breathe more asbestos naturally than this project will create, but I know that is not the answer. Cost/benefits analysis -- who cares; efficiency/effectiveness -- who cares; no one is going to fight this battle. We did it by the book; the book just didn't have the answer. Was it done wrong? What is the impact down the road? The customer is always right!

As I struggled with this reality, my day dealt me an example that says it all -- but then maybe you had to be there. January 30, 1997, the first day of the spring semester, and my first call of the semester deals with a wet carpet. An animal cage washer, on the fourth floor, leaked and water damaged an office below (carpet, books, some files) -- not much damage compared to other floods over the years. When I went to investigate, I found the occupant vacillating between tears and rage. "This has happened before; it has been like this for years; when are you going to fix it?" she asks. "My carpet (a scrap that had obviously been there for years) is ruined (granted, the horse-hair matting did stink); my books are ruined, and my data got soaked." "This isn't what I wanted to find my first day back; I should have been told sooner," she said. Reasonable requests, but just "another customer" until I discovered she was a Ph.D. student and some of the files contained data for her dissertation. All of a sudden, her problem became a little more personal. What went wrong? Why couldn't it be prevented? Why wasn't it fixed before? Nothing went wrong, yet everything went wrong. It was a small problem in the overall scheme of things, but the only problem from her perspective, and I could identify with her.

As you try to make sense of this world, as I try to understand the perspective of those on the outside looking in, I return to my three levels of existence: the issues on the surface, those below the surface that govern the relationships, and finally, more deeply still, my inner conflicts. I find that the surface issues dominate my thoughts, perhaps understandably, since it is on the surface that I am judged, and since my make-up, my being is driven to solve the problem. I want me to plug in a value for x in the equation and come out with the right answer, the only answer. The need for a single answer, the only answer is understandable. Everyone wants certainty; everyone wants simple solutions, but we are dealing with complex issues. Yet to the customer their problems should be easy to solve. There is no facility problem that can't be fixed if we apply enough resources to it, but that is part of the frustration on the surface. If I applied all of my resources to fixing that one roof, it would be fixed. But what about all the other roofs? There are not enough of us to go around. On the surface the various needs are fairly easy to understand, perhaps not to meet, but surely to understand. The customers on the receiving end of our services want us to be invisible; they want things to work. They:

- expect things to work well, all the time;

- want a fast permanent fix to facility problems, one that doesn't inconvenience them;

- want a new requirement supported quickly, cheaply, and with quality. They see a lack of responsiveness as a failure in supporting the institution's mission;

- don't want to be told it can't be done. They see "no" as an insensitive and inadequate orientation to their needs;

- aren't interested in my problems or how it is done. They don't understand the process and feel they have little control over the system that is supposed to meet their needs;

- see physical plant as an ineffective bureaucracy that could solve the problem if we "managed" properly. Few of them went as far as the professor who accused me of being stupid, incompetent, or evil; but inefficient, obstructive, wasteful all come to mind. They want the customer to be the center of the process.

An unspoken word at this juncture is that they want these services to be cost effective (i.e., inexpensive); they want efficiency, since that seems to be the accepted measure of worth, for after all, that is the objective, isn't it? They seek accountability, measurability, oversight, control, and they must be able to eliminate the suggestion of subjectivity, for that leads to value judgments, disagreements, and questions. We get wrapped up in these attempts to prove we are efficient and effective – words that have become synonymous with good management. But the forces we are dealing with defy those simple answers. The conflicting priorities are real. The various priorities, the limited resources, the yearly budget, the short term perspective, these are all complexities that govern how the issues on the surface complicate my life. But they are not the issues that we need to understand. While they govern our days, they aren't the important ones. The issues that confront all of us are the lack of control we all feel, the disenchantment with the "system," and the realities of bureaucratic processes.

As I reflect on my conversations with my customers the work of Birnbaum (1988), Dill (1991), and others echo in my mind. Most of us feel at one time or another that we are outsiders that we are at the mercy of the system, that we have very little influence over the bureaucracy that is there to support us. Why doesn't the University do something about "you guys" is repeated over and over again by the frustrated researcher. My research brings in a lot of money to this institution and I have to give part of it to pay for your services. "Why can't you do your job?" he asks. He seemed powerless; all he could do was yell and threaten to call the president. "I have been here twenty years and it is always the same," he argues. I try to be positive; I want to tell him about the conflicting priorities, the staffing problems, but he cuts me off. "I've been told about your problems, but I can't do my research. This is unacceptable." The conversation never moved beyond that point. I understood his perspective; I could almost agree with it, but what was I to do? We needed to solve his problem, but I don't have the resources to fix everyone's problem. As I left his office, in the bowels of one of the oldest buildings on campus, I sought answers. Is he influential enough to force the system to react to his frustration? It hasn't worked before. Why was I compelled to seek him out and listen to his complaints? If I don't do something, I will be reinforcing his belief that the maintenance people are incompetent, that nothing changes, and that the system is unresponsive. I vow to send someone over to look at the problem but I know all he will be able to do is "tweak" the system; the real solution is to replace the building and that is not going to happen. Why does his criticism affect me? Why do I want to show him that we can be responsive? My frustration equals his. His one example of poor service has grown into twenty years of poor service, and it will be used as one more nail in our coffin. The examples are everywhere; the practice is as ageless as the profession. My critics, my supporters, the ones assigned the task of "dealing" with physical plant share their frustrations and their pleas to have someone improve the maintenance organization's performance. Change the culture, become customer oriented, empower the employee, be responsive, fix the age-old problems, communicate -- all recommended actions, actions that cannot solve.

As we strive to deal with these issues we fall back to things we can measure. Numbers of work orders and response times are important, but they don't represent the real conflicts. Over the years I've been expected to believe that there is no conflict between and among the players that can't be resolved, or is that solved? Re-solved, does that mean solved, or does resolved simply mean solved again? Partnering, strategic planning, agreed-upon goals and objectives, the list goes on forever. Have I failed to use these tools to solve the problems on the surface? Am I at fault? Perhaps not, for I have discovered there are others who can shed light on my pain, who can help me put my struggles in perspective.

While I can understand that the conflicts are inevitable, I need to accept there are no mathematical answers. I have to accept that facilities are here to fade into the background, to serve. I have to shift resources to meet short notice needs. I have to realize that attention to details and constant juggling is required. I have to accept that the many players have their own agenda, and while we agree on the overall objectives, we define those objectives differently, and mostly assuredly we don't agree on how to achieve them. More importantly, I have to accept that resolving problems is not the same as solving them; that resolving doesn't mean making them go away. Instead, re-solving means continually solving again and this world will create frustration for my customers as well as for me, because none of us have control over the processes that influence our lives. The term "permanent white water" has been coined by Vaill (1989) to describe the complex, turbulent, changing environment in which we are trying to operate. Further, he suggests this environment has led to a lack of direction, an absence of coherence, and a loss of meaning, of control. Vaill notes that white water events contain a clash of logistics and priorities as asserted by various stakeholder groups such as customers, suppliers, owners, competitors, and employees, and that systems that were supposed to produce more control produced whole new kinds of problems that did not exist before. These events are not going to abate; they are going to get worse. Interestingly enough, the customer is also in permanent white water and would like a service supplier not to add to it, and preferably to reduce it. Vaill (1989) suggests that service has come to mean a willingness to absorb the customer's white water. That is a scary thought; what if the real determination of service turns out to be this unrelenting commitment? I am so focused on solving the problem that I have failed to see how my world fits into the whole. Short term needs drive decisions; conflicting priorities demand compromise; cost/benefit analysis sounds good in theory but the cost of a perception, the cost of the loss of power, of influence, far outweighs the benefit of an engineering solution. MBO, strategic planning, process re-engineering will not change that reality. "We are at our best when no one notices us." I recall Val Peterson's conclusion. I (we) provide a service and the value of that service, from the customer's perspective, is measured not by how much we do but by what we have not done. As I visit customers that I haven't seen for a while, I joke that either they have given up on calling me or that everything is OK. The implied conclusion is that they must have given up trying to get their problems fixed, for surely there must be problems, for surely there must be a lack of service. In reality, my success is in being like the Maytag repairman, since, as the commercial argues, the Maytag machines are so good that the repairman is unnecessary. I am at my best when I am not needed. The customer wants to be able to teach, to conduct research, to have the environment support his needs without that environment complicating his world. Responsiveness, flexibility, solving problems, and meeting needs are all indications of our ability to support the customer's perspective, his being, without being visible. But there are too many customers to support; we do not provide the same product to all. If our only measure of success were the cost (in purely a monetary sense) of our product, life would be easy. Unfortunately, parts of the "system" want economical service, others want socially acceptable service, still others want environmentally sound service, and then there are those who want to ensure the service being provided to others is accomplished in accordance with their rules, regulations, policies, procedures, conventions, and guidelines. My job security is assured. Someone must be able to balance all those conflicting needs, desires, and expectations. As I manipulate, as I influence, as I bend to keep on an even keel, what am I doing to the ones who work for me? They need and want stability; they need and want to control their world. Am I complicating their lives by trying to uncomplicate the customers'?

The reality that perception trumps the facts can be seen every day. The after-math of a natural disaster highlights this reality.

After a "once in a life time storm," power had been restored to the campus so we opened for business. Unfortunately power was still out in many of the surrounding communities (generating a lot of complaints… how are we supposed to come to class, or work, if we don't have any power). To add additional complications many of the traffic signals were still out causing traffic problems at the campus entrances. After receiving numerous complaints, the Vice President wanted to go to one of the intersections to see the problem for himself. I accompanied him (I told him crews were in the area working to restore the power) and we came upon a crew with several trucks working in and around the intersection. The Vice President wanted to talk to the person in charge, to impress upon him the importance of getting the power back on since it was a problem for the campus's traffic. Since I was "one of them," he asked me to find the person he could talk to (or was it, at).

I found the foreman, leaning over the hood of his truck with a coffee cup in hand, with several days of beard growth and a very obvious look of fatigue. We exchanged hello's, I asked him how long he had been up (for over 36 hours), and I acknowledged his efforts and the efforts of his crew. I told him that our Vice President wanted to talk to him. I shared with him what he wanted and he responded that he really didn't have the time and that they were about to energize the circuit. I told him I understood, and that I apologized for giving him any additional grief but that I would appreciate it if he could take a minute.

He agreed; the Vice President came over and started telling him how inconvenient this was and that he expected better service, and that he might have to complain to the power company's president. The foreman showed a lot more constraint than I expected, or that I would have. He simply said he would do all that he could. As we turned around I heard the foreman give the all clear, the circuits were energized and the lights came on. Our Vice President smiled, with a "see the influence I have" look on his face. I just gave a salute to the crew. They were off in a second, to head to the next problem, to listen to more complaints, to hear more demands for better service, knowing that they will be doing it all over again after the next storm.

Similarly after a tornado ripped through the campus I got a call from the President's house (he was having a meeting) notifying me that they had lost power. I was told to get hold of the Power Company and insist they get the power back on. After all we were one of their biggest customers; we were the University. I told the facility manager to tell the President that one of our smaller buildings had been destroyed and that we were pulling people out of the rubble. I wasn't in a position to make any phone calls right then. Perception versus reality!

The reality is, reality doesn't matter. Perceptions do. What a sad state of affairs. I am constantly amazed that intelligent people accept hearsay, unfounded statements, opinions, as fact. The old saying, "Don't let the facts stand in the way of a good story," rings true. I don't want to sound completely negative, I don't want stereotypes to govern my reality but that is what I have seen. I'm not proud of the fact that success demands manipulation, demands "working the system," demands taking risks and being criticized even if things "work" out. The realities of middle management are universal and ageless. People want things to be black and white, they want life to be uncomplicated, they want answers, they want control over their environment, they want stability, they want security, they want (and often need) more money, they want their life to be uncomplicated both in their personal and work life. Unfortunately, none of that is going to happen. Worse yet, the people they deal with have different goals and objectives, perceptions govern actions and reactions. Providing the rationale for a decision really doesn't matter if the decision does not support them.

Given this environment, these realities, we need to really understand where the "worker" is coming from. After all, they are the ones who do the work. They are the ones we are supposed to lead. They are the ones that you are supposed to motivate, mentor, train (educate), understand, guide, disciple, if necessary, in a positive way, listen to, reward, and rely on to get the job done. Leadership vice management is often defined as getting things done through people. It is our job to get the job done but it is those who work for us who really do the work. If we are going to be successful in our job we better understand where the employees, the workers, are coming from.

The study of the "work force" is fascinating. There is no question that over time the expectations have changed. The skills required have changed, technology has changed how we do things, and technology has created new jobs, and has eliminated others. However, for the foreseeable future there will still be people who work with their hands, and in most cases they are dedicated, skillful, and productive. On the other hand there are those who are not. My experience is no different from yours. There are good employees (whatever that means), and there are bad employees. We know the difference, we know who we rely on, we know who doesn't pull their weight but quantifying it, measuring the difference, is not easy. What makes an outstanding ground keeper, what is the difference between meets expectations and exceeds expectations. I can talk it, I can know it, but don't tell me you can quantify it.

CHAPTER IV
THE PERSPECTIVE OF THE WORKER

Those on the outside and those who support the ones swinging the hammer have their view, but what about the ones in the trenches? Who speaks for them? As policies and procedures are implemented, as consultants tell management how to deal with the "work" force, as we do what is best for the organization, do we really listen to the workers? The workers--what an interesting choice of words. Does that imply that the ones on the sidelines, the ones directing the show, don't work? As we spend hours upon hours measuring their productivity, perhaps it is appropriate for them to ask how productive we are as we sit in meeting after meeting! We seem to spend an inordinate amount of time trying to improve the "work" of the workers.

Do we remember what it's like to walk in the employee's shoes? Have you ever been there? I've probably spent more time in the trenches than most of the ones telling me how to provide better service, but even the time I've spent is limited. I'm on the edge of the hole to show support, I plow snow to relieve the stress of my "regular" job, but I don't do the work for a living. I don't live in the technician's or the custodian's shoes. I recall but two memories from my days of shooting screws on an assembly line. The first was the desire to stay busy, to work fast, and to see how much I could get done even though the permanent employees didn't like this temporary college student making them "look bad." An effort to understand the dynamics of that exchange would take volumes, but regardless of who was responsible for the environment, there was no question that we were looking at the job with different perspectives. The other memory is of spelling my girlfriend's (now my wife's) name in the glue I used to attach the nameplates to the machines. I wonder if any of those dishwashers are still in use. If someone peeled off the nameplate, I wonder if they would see "Connie" spelled out.

The question for me is not what should be done to make employee's job more meaningful or fulfilling; it is not about empowerment, job enlargement, or labor/management relations. The question we need to ask is, "Can we see our world through the eyes of those who work for us?" What forces influence their path? We have different perspectives, different agendas. Do we honestly believe we can share the same goals and objectives? I conducted a survey a number of years ago and recall that an employee asked: "Why conduct surveys pretending you are interested in our input when you actually have no intention of following through with any action? I think this survey was just a feel–good thing, to make the workers think Jack actually cares about what we think." How can I let that comment roll off my back? Another employee response to an endless stream of surveys: "This survey does not address the real problems; if you want to know the real problems just ask."

As we communicate the need to be more business-like, we are told it is nothing but calls for more work with no increase in pay. We tell employees that pay for merit programs are designed to reward good people, are a solution to unfairness, are designed to be objective measures so we can deal with their concern about favoritism and the "good old boy network," but the employees are not accepting our arguments. What are we missing? We look at the relationship from our perspective, but the employees are looking at it from theirs. The programs, conceived and implemented by those on the outside, are advertised to meet the needs of the employees, but they miss the mark. We profess to be concerned about the worker's needs, but we measure our success by judging our ability to meet our customers' needs and the demands of those who provide the resources. Can the two sides come together? Do we all have the same goals in mind? Can we use the rules of the private sector to govern the public sector? Is the private sector the answer to our problems, or do the solutions depend upon one's perspective? Am I the enemy? Over the years I've celebrated with the employees as they overcame obstacles, as they worked through the night to fix a broken water main. But, this success is quickly overshadowed by what wasn't accomplished.

I think about the individuals who stand out in my mind over the years and most have common characteristics. They have risen through the ranks because of technical expertise; they worked hard when they were young, but the construction industry had taken its toll and they move slower now. They had grown up in an environment where loyalty was cherished. They took care of their own, but one earned his rights by doing the dirty work. The successful ones had their own businesses and made as much money on the side as they did on their "government" job, but they had all grown tired. However, when the chips were down they gave their all. Frank Dalli stands as a beacon. A demonstrative Italian, he grew up laying sewer pipe; he had the biggest hands and the biggest heart I have ever seen. As a supervisor he lacked "management skills" i.e., he wasn't very diplomatic; he couldn't or wouldn't look at the big picture, but when there was a sewer break he would be the first in the hole. With sewage covering his wing tips he would fix the problem. The OSHA inspectors today would have a fit: no shoring, no safety equipment. He did everything wrong, except fixing the problem. These same heroics take place today. I recall a computer skilled HVAC technician with his arms thrust above his head as 140 degree water streamed over his body as he attempted to find a value to prevent flooding a laboratory. I see workers battling snow storms, hurricanes, floods, and any number of other crises, but there are also those who never go beyond their job description, and who complain constantly about their wages and that management (me) doesn't support them. Am I to treat all of these the same? Is "same" the equivalent of "equal?" How do I differentiate between and among employees? One of the "old timers," a senior member of management, remarks: "What do you people want? So what if we don't get all the paperwork done. So what if we don't follow all the rules. So what if we are protecting Joe. He was a great worker but he can't handle the tough jobs now so we let him work around the shop. Our job is watching out for the employees. When there is a problem they are there, isn't that what it is all about?" Perhaps that is what it is all about and when the chips are down they are there. But it doesn't seem to be enough. Frank Dalli fixed the sewer breaks. He did not like the politics. He didn't like yielding to the "bigger" picture. He didn't like supporting the team if it meant less support for his people. He was unbelievable but he wasn't a good manager, at least from management's perspective.

How do we tell those who work for us how important they are, how important the job they are doing is, while at the same time knowing that even if their hard work is recognized, the praise won't last long. As proud as I am of what is accomplished, I know that one mistake wipes out all the "Atta boys." Why can't I accept the reality that what has been accomplished is no longer an issue? I understand the customers' perspective that the current problem is the one they want solved. However, I can't accept the complaint that we should have finished today's job last week; last week we were working on an earlier panic. Do I explain to the customer that we have other customers, other priorities? Do I tell the customer how many employees are out sick every Friday? Do I tell the customer my problems? I'd like to but it doesn't do any good. I think back to that last trip around my base in England--and it was my base, not my boss's, not the Air Force's, not some piece of land with buildings on it. It was mine. I spent three years, literally every day, often all day and many nights, working to improve the facilities. I saw everything that had been accomplished--countless hours, sweat, tears, and most certainly some blood was shed, but my replacement and his new boss only saw what needed to be done. They had their perspective; they didn't see, and had no reason to see, mine. When the water is running down the street it does one little good to stand there and say, "We told you it was installed wrong." "We told you that saving money at first would cost more at the end." No one cares; stopping the water is the only thing that is important. But what do I say to the technician who gets pulled from one job to put his finger in the dike. He knows he will get complaints from the customer he just left, and he knows he will get complaints about this job. I don't care what the books say about vision statements, shared objectives, empowerment, accountability, efficiency, for many it is "just a job," it is about surviving. Nothing ties the demands of the outside world to the frustrations of the ones in the trenches more that the emphasis on increasing productivity, on accountability, on doing more with less. Be more business-like, is the decree. The customers expect it, the legislators demand it, the public is convinced it will make the public sector work more effectively, and management consultants all say it is our salvation. Amazing--twenty years ago we had a saying, "We are doing more and more with less; pretty soon we will be doing everything with nothing." Some things never change.

Surely the employees should be able to see the handwriting on the wall and should want to participate in efforts to improve service, accomplish more, and become more customer-oriented. Do we really believe they will understand? Do we expect them to help us eliminate their jobs? Don't worry, we'll retrain them, is the answer. Not very comforting to a person who has no computer skills, who has been doing the same job for twenty-five years, who is looking for retirement, not stress. I've talked until I was blue in the face. I've written newsletters. We've created teams of workers to come up with ways to do more, and the word on the street is "Baker" is out to get us. From my vantage point, all I'm doing is asking people to do is work and get the job done. What have I done wrong? A foreman, organizationally a member of management, is livid and states very emphatically, "You've said we have to be multi-skilled technicians; that is what will make the department more efficient. Ok, I'm multi-skilled - promote me, pay me more money," "I change light bulbs in mechanical rooms. I look for problems in all trades as I walk through a building. I deserve to be multi – skilled and make more money." Wait a minute, you've got to be joking, I think. You need to do more work, you need to be a team member, you need to challenge those who aren't carrying their weight. "Do you really believe what you do is meeting the criteria?" I ask. "I need more money" is his response. What do I say to the technician who tells me he doesn't believe a word management says? "I believe what I believe" is his response; "nothing you say will change my mind." I can't compete with that. Since he believes he does work out of his trade (not according to his job description) he believes he should be multi-skilled--even though I can have others do the work to eliminate the conflict, but he doesn't want to hear that. Most of this work is done on overtime so he wants to do the work; he just wants more money to do it. I'm tempted to tell him he can't have his cake and eat it too, but why not?

You're taking our overtime! Every conversation with a maintenance mechanic sooner or later turns to the subject of money and overtime. No other topic better represents my frustration and the tensions between my worlds. It is difficult to understand the issue of money and its power over the relationships. Over the years the concept that money does not motivate has been beaten into me. The motivation theories (Herzberg, 1967; Maslow, 1978) suggest that more money only satisfies for a little while, and then you want more again. The argument is that I should stress job satisfaction, intrinsic rewards, a well-deserved thanks. I do all those things, but we always return to money. As I stress productivity, as I stress managing overtime, a supervisor responds:

"My men need overtime, they don't make enough money.
If I can get them overtime that's what I do."

We certainly aren't striving for the same goal. I begin my cost-cutting, efficiency argument, but the supervisor responds: The trades are underpaid; they have not had a pay raise in years. I can't reward the hard workers, they all need second jobs. If they take second jobs, then they won't be available when I need them. Morale is shot and you want me to take away their overtime. I can't do that."

I begin the speech I am expected to give, the one my management side believes: "People should not rely on overtime. You can't assume you will get overtime." I say it but I know it fall on deaf ears. I reflect on what I know my bosses would say: "Their job description says they have to be available in case of an emergency--we can make them respond." I know those are the rules but what if they call in sick? Well, the rules say I can ask for documentation "if" I suspect abuse. How much time do I spend chasing this problem? It is a full time job and if this issue is put to bed another will take its place. It's easy to stand behind the rules when it's not your responsibility to get the job done. It's easy to say that's the way it should be. If I say no to the employees and then can't respond to an emergency, I wonder if anyone will remember our decision to play hard ball? Not in my experience; the emergency will be the only topic of conversation. I run the conversations through my mind after talking to the employees. I don't know how they pay their bills. I don't know why they should see the benefits of the state system. I don't know how to get beyond the pay issues and emphasize productivity issues. I understand their frame of reference, but I'm supposed to support the system.

As "management" seeks ways to improve performance and productivity we rediscover the idea that rewards (money) should be tied to performance. While much of the literature suggests that an employee's pay should be tied to overall performance of the company; that gets a little hard to do in public sector. How do I tie a carpenter's performance to the outcome of an institution of higher education? Do we even know what the outcomes are, let alone the relationship between them and a carpenter's pay? On one hand we stress teamwork; on the other we plan to reward outstanding individual performance. We are speaking out of both sides of our mouths again. A new pay plan, providing an opportunity to grant "double increments" (based on performance) is implemented. A new performance plan (providing a method to identify the outstanding performance) is developed, and neither is accepted as advertised--what is going on? Do the employees agree with the proposal? Most agreed with the concept-pay for "good" performance--but there just isn't any agreement on how to define "good." What a frustrating situation. What a beautiful example of conflicting goals, objectives, and perspectives. The direction was to implement a new performance (employee evaluation) plan; after all, the public is demanding accountability, demanding that we be more productive. Intuitively, it make sense, but those expectations run headlong into the ageless problem all performance plans face: objective versus subjective criteria. The proponents of the theory talked about objective measures such as inspections, customer surveys, and standards. We saw the training film and counted errors in a letter, missed appointments, answering the phone before the third ring--all things we could measure, but as I talked to employees, reality struck.

What makes a grounds keeper outstanding? Do you measure the easy things like lateness? Do you measure the end results of this effort, how good the grounds look? Do you rate him outstanding if the flowerbeds look great? What about if the grass is too long? What is the right length for grass? The pat answer is to do inspections, but the employees ask: "what determines if a bed looks good?" If it has no weeds in it. How about ten weeds per bed? Is that for a week, a month, always? Those were all questions asked. We said we were going to be objective, but are we really going to count weeds? Then the employee asked the really tough question: "You know, we are told over and over again how good the campus looks. The President always compliments us in every speech, and visitors fall in love with the grounds. Obviously we are doing an outstanding job, all of us deserve a raise. Why don't you give us all a raise?" We sold the concept to the employees as a way to reward performance, but how are we going to measure it? The grounds look good, but we know that not everyone is outstanding. We will make subjective evaluations. Why did we say it would be objective?

How do you measure "foster teamwork?" Even though there are surveys to conduct, customer complaints to count, what is the difference between "outstanding teamwork," and "exceeds expectations teamwork?" How do you measure cleanliness of a restroom? "Wipe the wall down once a day" can be measured (if you're standing there); determining whether it is <u>clean</u> is a judgment. What is the quality of a roof repair? Does it leak? No! So is that outstanding? What are the standards for an outstanding roof patch?

As I talked to a new employee, he reinforces the typical stereotypes. "State workers would never make it on the outside. They don't know how well off they are." He continued, "We didn't get the holidays they do. If there wasn't work we didn't get paid. If you came in late you were fired." His frustrations were evident. The mixed signals, the lack of clear direction, the procurement laws, the expenditure of a dime to save a nickel were almost too much for him to handle. "On the outside your success is based on establishing relationships with your suppliers, the vendors that support you," he stated. "The state's low-bid mentality doesn't allow that to happen; it costs money," he argues. Many of his examples were true and even from my perspective; much of what we do seems wasteful, especially as we clamor to "be more businesslike." The transition into the public sector for a construction worker, or even worse, for a tradesperson who had his own business, is a traumatic experience. My new employee couldn't believe the frequent use of sick leave; he complained about the steps that one had to go through to get material and the almost unbelievable effort put into employee evaluations, employee development, employee complaints. On the outside you work, you work hard, or you're out of work, was his perspective. The question remains, and the bets are down. When will he become acclimated to "our way of business?" What a pessimistic, depressing thought. Is this the only option? Why can't his perspective become ours? It's back to blaming the system. My hero of old, Frederick Taylor, and his scientific method (time studies, mass production, etc.) takes the blame. But perhaps it goes back to perspective. I don't want to debate which system is better, which system places more value on the person, which system is best; let it suffice that the two systems have some differences and some similarities. In either case, one's perspective depends on which side of the fence he is on.

When I'm stressing productivity and the big picture, the employees don't see me as being on their side, but I see both sides and it is pulling me apart. After spending hours in the hot sun, is a break acceptable? Of course it is. Is sleeping in the mechanical room all day acceptable? Of course it's not. Is pulling someone off a job to handle an emergency acceptable? Of course it is. Is pulling off the job because you don't get along with your supervisor acceptable? Of course it's not. It is easy to figure out the extremes.

It's that huge gray area in the middle that no one agrees on. It's that gray area that is fraught with judgments, inconsistencies; it is the area that you have to live in to understand. Following rules is easy; deciding how to bend them is tough, but to be successful you must. What do the employees want me to do?

The retirement of two of plant's oldest employees provides some powerful lessons for those who are pushing productivity, accountability, a more business-like environment. At one end of the spectrum is a longtime supervisor -- an articulate, worldly, deeply devoted family man (his own and plant's) who speaks of the good old days and of his future, traveling with his wife. On the other end is an employee, who after working for the organization for 42 years finds himself with no place to go. He speaks little and wonders why he has to leave. Both paint a picture of what they are going to miss and what they want me to do. The supervisor talked about his friends, he remembered the emergencies, and he talked about people helping people. He had little to say about the new emphasis on productivity; instead he wanted me to remember that people are important. He reminisced about a wheelchair that mysteriously found its way around plant only to end up at the front door of the department's "head" guy. He knew that would be frowned upon now; I didn't ask him if the chair had been delivered in a state truck. He talked about when he was sick and some friends came out to help shovel and sand his front sidewalk; he didn't say it but we both knew they were on the clock. He told about employees helping employees, and reflected sadly that that didn't happen anymore. I know we tend to see the past with rose-colored glasses, but these were more than just isolated instances. The organization had lost its sense of family as far as he was concerned. There is too much stress today, too much emphasis on getting the job done at the expense of people. The few job-related issues he talked about sent shivers down my spine. He told me about responding to an elevator call only to find the car going up and down, up and down with people screaming inside. He stopped it by shoving a screwdriver in the control panel. He talked about helping a professor fix a fume hood, only to be overcome by cyanide gas. Ironically, just a few days earlier I had been chastised for our slow response in fixing a fume hood -- our current procedure requires getting the hood cleared by environmental safety. You can argue we should have someone standing by to clear hoods (and fix heating problems in dorms) but it is hard to argue about taking extra steps after talking to this gentleman. One begins to wonder was it so much better in the "old days;" maybe we were less efficient, maybe we were "firemen" (i.e., when it broke, we were there), maybe that was our measure of success.

The other employee's perspective was just as unique. He entered employment as a laborer, left as a foreman. His entire life was spent on this campus. He had witnessed tremendous changes, tremendous stability. Although he can neither read nor write, he accepted every challenge; he willingly took on the dirtiest job. But he was expected to supervise, a task requiring skills he never had the opportunity to learn. Often criticized by younger employees for his willingness to do management's bidding; his quiet, unassuming ways won over many. He had a smile as big as all outdoors. Had the system used him, as some would suggest? He seemed proud of the work he had done, but his perspective was limited. He had strong memories of being an outcast when he first arrived on campus, but he stuck it out. Two sons had graduated from college, his sacrifices made it possible. None of his comments dealt with management, accountability, the role of higher education, conflicting priorities, or making decisions; he simply did what his boss told him to do. He was one of the last to be promoted for his technical skills alone. He did the work; he didn't lead those who worked for him. It wasn't his fault, it wasn't his role. There was nobody I trusted more; fixing a roof in a thunderstorm was his job, no ands, ifs, or buts. He recalled that life was tough back then that younger employees don't understand. But life is still tough.

I reflect on a conversation I had with an employee whose paycheck for two weeks was thirty-five dollars. After being off for two days without pay while he worked a side job (he didn't realize he wouldn't be getting paid leave even though he had no leave built up after fifteen years), after child support, and without overtime (he had lost his driver's license so he had no way of working late), he walked out with thirty-five dollars. To further complicate his life he had just been cleaned out by the people he had been sharing a room with and he owed money to a number of others. I reflect on the comments made at a recent retirement party. The retiree was praised because he had found employees overtime when things were tough; that was some twenty years ago but the need is still there. How do you compete with this perspective? Granted, the past usually looks better than it was, and we all have the ability to remember the good things, not the bad, but it seems that most believe the past provided things that today's workplace doesn't.

- We've lost our sense of family. It's more than not having shop parties (even though there were some wild ones); people worked together more. It is cut-throat now, a retired supervisor recalls.

- Management doesn't care about us. We need pay raises; you are taking our overtime away. I have to have overtime to pay the bills, a mechanic laments.

- We came to the University because of the security, the benefits, but they aren't any better than private industry and their salaries are better – comments from an HVAC technician who is contemplating leaving.

- We did our job back then, there weren't all the committees, you did what the boss said (retiree).

There is no question that looking back was done with rose-colored glasses. There were others who didn't reflect on the past very fondly. They gave examples of the "good old boy network," there were stories of favoritism, of being an outcast, of unfairness. I'm sure that was true but I hear the same complaints today.

The blue-collar worker, the trades, semi-skilled labor--it is almost as if they have been declared an endangered species. As I scan the library shelves I find row after row of books describing the plight of oil riggers, the steelworkers, and perhaps most poignantly, the coal miners, with graphic pictures of claustrophobic, filthy working conditions. But the stories seem to end around the 1950s, almost as if the conditions were mysteriously eliminated. The texts shifted to the work of white--collar workers, to the technical workplace of the future (now) with its emphasis on empowering the employees, the service industry, management, leadership, the information age, and an environment of workers who are the enterprise. Have we forgotten the laborer? Has he truly become obsolete? Has he become transformed? As I become absorbed in seeing, intellectually as well as visually, the transition in the literature, I reflect on the realities of my world. Although there has been some progress, the work is not as dirty or as dangerous as it was. Standing in sewage today is not all that much different from doing it twenty years ago. We are not the workforce, the enterprise that is being championed as the workforce of the future. We are miles away from self-motivation, from sharing the vision, from measuring our performance as an integral part of the institution's mission. During those times that I'm not walking a tightrope, I'm straddling a large chasm between the workplace of the future and the workplace of the past.

The blue-collar worker is quite an enigma. Charles Spencer's (1977) <u>Blue</u> <u>Collar</u> is about workers, workers who in his words are not those exceptional souls for whom work is an aesthetic's reward, but rather about the plain, obscure, everyday worker for whom work is the only choice: skilled, semi-skilled workers and how they make it in the workplace. It is about their daily hassles over working conditions, their beefs and grievances against a boss, their union loyalties and frustrations, and their periodic encounters with work ethic. It is also about bosses, not Harvard School of Business renditions, rather authentic management people, checking, recording, and clearly forgetting if required, maintaining discipline and making tough decisions. As the stories of the "rank and file," of the third or fourth generation laborer, of the one in the trenches are told, realities don't conform to management's desire to be more productive, to be more accountable, to be more management-like. One finds that seniority is a treasured expectation--it is my turn because I've put in my time. One finds that job security, stability, and predictability are important. Benefits that are now being threatened are seen as fundamental rights. One finds employees whose goal is to be a forklift operator instead of a laborer because it is easier on his back. It is a status symbol, it pays more money; it has nothing to do with increased responsibility or personal growth.

Mine is not the world of self-actualization (Maslow, 1978). As I talk to a team leader (he would never call himself a supervisor) of a group of computer programmers, he notes that office parties don't create much interest; his employees would rather stay at their computers. I wonder what he thought when I told him my employees saw the parties as a free meal, maybe the best they had all week, and a free afternoon off since they could unofficially leave at 1 p.m. As I searched for support of my argument that maintenance is often overlooked, I found Hoffer's (1969) Working and Thinking on the Waterfront, an often quoted text on our failure to maintain. While I fully support his concern about the failure to maintain, I marvel at his pronouncement that "thinking is used as an escape from working. Eight hours palletizing short 4 by 4s on Pier 48B. The easiest, steadiest, and most wearisome job I have ever known. Time flew, but the leaden monotony was frightening. There was no pause to sit down or catch one's breath. I refused to return to it tomorrow." Page after page, day after day, ship after ship, the worker was dispatched and he escaped by thinking. I cannot begin to know what it is like to put in eight hours and treat work as something that must be endured. To spend time trying to escape, by thinking, or by playing, or perhaps by drinking. Perhaps those who argue that work is a natural desire forget that the work one loves may not be one's job. I feel guilty in agreeing with Spencer's characterization of the work force I know. For more than twenty years I've been told that the workforce I deal with on a daily basis doesn't need to be that way, that management is holding it back, that it needs to be transformed, that it needs to change. Yet over all these years the best and worst of the blue-collar worker remains, at least in my world.

I have tried to look at my world from the employees' vantage point, but I have looked through my eyes. Can I see what they see? I have always assumed that what is good for the organization is good for the employee. Do the employees agree with that perspective? What do employees want? Their words hit me across the face: "We don't believe you are supporting us." "You need to get the system to support us." "We deserve pay raises." When the chips are down, they pull together--why do they pull apart other times? The employees, much like our customers, want communications but their perspective is different. They didn't talk about getting the job done; they wanted to know what was going to affect them, on a very personal level. They felt that the mechanisms used to pass on information were limited, that information was not passed on quickly enough and that communication in general needed to be improved. But then there was the most damning of all. A mechanic stated: "There is a perception among employees that management is secretive or hiding information. That failure to receive information in a timely fashion is perceived as purposeful, contrived, antagonistic behavior designed to exclude us from information about training and/or promotional opportunities." That comment cut me to the core. What are we doing wrong? We talk at length about what we are about. There are newsletters, weekly staff meetings, newspapers, a hotline. What aren't we communicating? It can't be just about training, and it is easy to find out about vacancies. There has to be more. It ends up they want answers where there are none. Perhaps it is human nature, perhaps it is a concrete frame of reference, but they want to know: "What is my future?" "Will we get a pay raise?" Why is that new building going up when you say the system can't afford cost-of living increases?" "Why can't you change my job classification, you took care of his?" "Why can't you convince the legislature that the electrical job has to move forward?" "Why wasn't I selected for the job?"

The employee' inability to control their own destiny and their desire for rational decision affects how they see the world. They say they don't trust management. They say they are not treated fairly, but do we even agree on the terminology? Trust is often equated to "you said 'X' several months ago; now you are saying 'Y' . . . you lied to us." It doesn't matter that things changed during that time. Fairness is used interchangeably with the same. Why do we have to punch a time clock and management doesn't -- it's not fair. Why do office workers get to take a break when they want it and we have to schedule ours? Why do I have to come in and shovel snow when others do not? Why is everyone else getting a pay raise and I (or we) are not? Why am I being disciplined when he/she did the same thing and nothing happened to him/her? Why was the steamfitter sitting next to a tree, yet my supervisor writes me up when I do? None of this seems fair. Why indeed. The steamfitter had just spent twenty minutes in a four-by-six foot steam vault, 15 feet underground, with temperatures exceeding 100 degrees. Maybe that's why he is taking a break, but that part of the story isn't told.

What do I say to the employee who complains: "We are called in for snow removal operations; we fight the highways when everyone else stays home. When we get there you send us home an hour after we arrive." I explain it stopped snowing and everything had turned to ice. We can't shovel ice and we can't afford to have 200 employees sitting around drawing overtime when there is no work to do. It's not fair, but that's the job. Fair treatment, equal treatment: are these one and the same? It seems that many of the concerns expressed by employees were based on these concepts. Equal seemed to translate to fair. If everyone is treated the same, then suggestions of favoritism, of the "good old boy" network, of unfairness would be eliminated.

But is fair "equal?" Is equal "fair?" It is hard to argue with those who want employees to be treated the same, given the same, or equal, circumstances. Once again, I find myself questioning this black or white view of the world. Circumstances are seldom, if ever, the same. Sameness seems to come up every time an employee is questioned about his performance, or is disciplined because of some transgression against the rules, policies, or procedures. Sameness is linked to fairness, which is linked to morale, trust, equality and the absence of any, or all, of these concepts is management's (my) responsibility. But life is not necessarily fair; as trite as that may sound, it's true. An employee provides his example (one employee is suspended, another is not, supposedly for the same offense) and I give mine (a steamfitter leaning against the tree after coming out of a steam vault is not the same as a carpenter leaning against that same tree). We are not even talking the same language. I resort to my "parent" mode--don't worry about everyone else, just worry about what you do. I admit there are times when I treat people differently. Hopefully that doesn't equate to "unfairly," but it <u>does</u> mean "not the same." When there is a crisis I am going to go to the one on whom I can rely, the one in whom I have confidence, the one I know will get the job done. When an employee who has no leave built up, who uses his leave the day it is accumulated, asks me to give him a day off, I will not think of him in the same way that I think of an employee who has never used a day of unscheduled leave. When a 60-year-old employee takes a break on his snow shovel, I doubt that I'll question it. When a 20-year-old takes the same number of breaks, I will. Is that the same? No. Is it fair? It depends on your perspective. Striking the balance between and among following the rules, bending the rules, breaking the rules is not easy, nor is it fun. Strict adherence to the letter of the law is the easiest way but is it the fair way? Is it the way that will get the job done?

The desire for fairness leads one to quantification, measurements, and comparisons. If the numbers prove there is a difference, no one can argue; numbers don't lie. We fall prey to the desire to take subjectivity out of the process. But I don't know how to do that. I understand the desire to do it. I appreciate it would make my life easier but the <u>desire</u> to do, and <u>ability</u> to do are different. Unfortunately, after we convince ourselves and the employees that quantification will solve the problems of fairness and equality, we fall into the trap of saying we do it. If we don't, our credibility suffers; there will be not trust. But can we agree with some measure of fairness? The spiral down continues. The suggestion of fair treatment, thus equal treatment, strikes at the very heart of performance appraisals. Yet, our efforts to quantify the process are met with complaints of favoritism, the "good old boy" network, unfairness, the very problems the process was designed to fix. We appear to be our own worst enemy. Peters (1985) suggests that the worst offenders of performance appraisals and job descriptions are in the public sector, and that programs developed at the turn of the century in response to the favoritism and corruption of the political machines of that era went too far. He suggests that most regulations, written in response to legislation or executive order (to deal with some transgression), amounts to killing a gnat with a sledgehammer. I couldn't agree more. We have created a monster and are trying to convince everyone it is good. Same is same, equal implies same, but does fair imply equal or same? We have convinced everyone that objectivity will solve all our problems. We have failed to remind ourselves that subjectivity is reality. Is there any wonder why we are accused of changing the story based on the audience?

I find myself on the tightrope again. We stress productivity and I'm accused of more work for no additional pay. Economically-sound decisions that are supported by analysis and engineering calculations, are changed because of political issues. A part of me accepts the conflicts, but part of me condemns the policies. A part of me wants to escape from the need to subjugate the needs and desires of those who work for me for the common good of the organization; but part of me realizes that the system will, and must, prevail. A part of me wants to tell the employees to just go to work; but part of me want to tell my bosses that they don't understand what goes on in the trenches. I have the ability, or is it the curse, to see both sides. I try to walk the fine line, but at times it is extremely hard to do. At times I fail.

How do you gain an understanding of those who come together to create the group of people who maintain facilities? These are people with different backgrounds, with different occupations, with different needs, desires and objectives. Yet we come together. I think of Frank Dalli. I think of those working around the clock to bring a base, a city, a community back to life after a snow storm, tornadoes, floods, or man-made disaster, and then I think of those who ride around in their trucks, or sleep in the mechanical room. I think of the ones who have stayed in the same job for 30 years. I count the many who have never graduated from high school, who know no other world. The stereotypes abound: key rings, greasy shirts, a "not my job" mentality. But then I think of family, of members fighting like brother and sister, members complaining that life is not fair, that their allowance is not enough, that those who are to care for them aren't protecting them. How do I characterize this group? Are we family or are we strangers just thrown together to do a job?

Those who do trade work certainly have a unique perspective. The term culture (Schein, 1982) can be used to explain why we are what we are, but it is also used to "explain" our bad habits, our inefficiency, our limited perspective and our failures. In the past, attempts to solve the problems of the "culture" have been made by restructuring it (i.e., changing the organizational structure); by trying to motivate it (empowering, delegating, and rewarding it); by giving it shared goals (or visions, or strategies); by managing it (through Total Quality Management, Management by Objective, etc.); and in some cases by "beating up on" it. Since those actions seemed to fail, it has been determined that it is time to change it. It seems we need to make it more business-like, but what does that mean? Is the existing culture bad, or does it just not meet the current expectations? Why has culture become the euphemism for everything that is preventing a facility maintenance organization from fitting the mold that our bosses and our customers want?

There have been very few, if any, attempts to understand the culture of a service organization. While there are many who declare that we should change it in order to shape it into an organization that meets our expectations, I see little attempt to understand it. Stereotypes seem to fit. The complaints of the customers seem to shape the view that we lack an appreciation for the customer's needs. We fail to communicate. We are unproductive. We lack an appreciation for workforce diversity (in other words we are a male dominated environment), and we have failed to keep up with the changing workplace. Those are all perceptions from the outside. I deal with a culture that demands loyalty; that values hard work when required, and that understands what it is like to be criticized at every turn. Certainly these are different perspectives. As I searched for other who identified with, who could understand the environment without wanting to mold into something different, I found a study on the significance of shop floor humor (Collinson, 1988). Although limited in scope, and certainly only a snapshot of my world, it comforted me; I am not alone. Collinson found that humor, at times very crude, was a crucial mechanism through which shop floor relations and practices were mediated and that the cultural identities contributed to shop floor cohesion, a shared sense of masculinity, and facilitated the worker's self-differentiation from and aversion to white collar staff and managers. As I turned each page I echoed the comments; he was describing us. But, he was describing a culture that has been declared obsolete. We have told an entire society that what has sustained them, what has established relationships, what has worked for years is no longer acceptable. We ask why our efforts are met with resistance.

Over forty years ago Argyris' (1957) interviews with assembly-line workers suggested they held a number of personal characteristics. He found that the workers perceived themselves as poorly educated. They disliked change, were rigid in attitude, placed emphasis on predictability and surety, and valued money most importantly with seniority second. I know his assessment will be challenged, but regardless of one's persuasion, Argyris' predicted reaction by management came to pass. To combat the assembly-line workers "attitudes," he expected management to call for stronger, more dynamic leadership, more management controls, and emphasis on "human relations." All of those reactions indeed came to pass, even though Argyris predicted the results would be a reinforcement of the original problems. Some forty years later I believe his predictions have proved correct. He concluded that formal organizational principles made demands of relatively healthy individuals which were incongruent with their needs and that frustration, conflict, and a short term perspective are predictable. One can debate the causes of this reality and his analysis, but his conclusions certainly describe my world.

I turned to Brown (1954) whose views on the importance of informal groups ring true as I reflect on my experience and my discussions of those who work for me. His discussions of the importance of the informal organization cannot be overlooked. He suggested that: "To predict the behavior of a plumber is not enough to know the expectations of the man who holds the carrot or the stick. Nor is it only a matter of the expectations of the officials of the plumber's union. We must also know the expectations of the plumber's mate." Brown goes on to state that it is evident that no amount of enlightened management can satisfy the worker if he feels that the social system of which he is a member is in some respects unfair. I think back to the employee who said, "I believe what I believe and nothing you can say will change that."

The few who have looked at workers in a "factory" environment, one that stresses manual labor, repetitiveness, limited flexibility, seem to gloss over their findings as they call for empowerment and more employee involvement. Even though any number of studies suggest workers are driven by a desperate inner urge to find a place to take root, seek an unofficial code which exerts a powerful influence over group members, are governed by attitudes that are conditioned by social demands from both inside and outside the workplace, and establish informal groups that exercise strong social controls over the work habits and attitudes of the individual (Brown, 1954), all seem to find these significant issues as nothing more than obstacles to be overcome by the latest management techniques. We never seem to step back and seek to understand. We seem bent on glossing over the issues, with the apparent belief that we can "manage" them, i.e., overcome, solve, and move beyond the complexities. That "solve mentality" seems to take charge. Is there any wonder why our efforts to mold the culture into one acceptable to management are met with resistance?

On the surface, we attempt to manipulate the culture to meet the needs of the customers; below the surface I want to understand. It appears that most of our effort is focused to promote more effective managerial action, to mold the culture to meet our objectives. To understand is to take a deeper look; to gain a broader understanding requires critical reflection upon an organization's life and work (Alvesson, 1993). Ouchi and Wilkins (1985) suggest that the contemporary student of organizational culture often looks for a rational instrument, designed by top management, to shape the behavior of the employees in purposeful way--ways related to effectiveness and performance. However, Martin and Meyerson (1985) suggest that culture is often best in terms of diverse, even contradictory, values and symbols and that the black hole in our definition of culture is the exclusion of ambiguity, uncertainty, contradiction and confusion. I again find myself looking for the easy answer, the way to get people to sign up to my view of the world. Manipulate, convince, show them the errors of their ways-- all come to mind. I mean to convince them that what has protected them in the past is no longer good for them. No longer good for the organization maybe, but are "the workers" the organization? The employees see family; the conversations ring in my ears. "I've lived with my men for twenty-five years," a supervisor laments. "They need the overtime to make ends meet. Don't take their overtime away--I need to protect them." How do I reconcile that with the arguments for better, cheaper service? The customer yells—"The university needs to do something about you guys," and the employees and their supervisors yell they want me to "do something" about improving their position in the organization. The perspective of those who retired, those who work two jobs the supervisors who see themselves on the side of the employee not management, those who see me as an outsider, those are the ones who deserve understanding.

The maintenance culture is more than the key rings and greasy shirts. At the core of every culture are assumptions about the proper way for individuals to relate to each other in order to make the group safe and comfortable (Schein, 1992). Alvesson (1993) suggest we should see culture as its expressive forms, manifestations of human consciousness, and that what underlies that idea of culture is hermeneutical or phenomenological, rather than objectivist. My world continues to get more complex. What do I do? Whose side am I on? I'm either with them or against them. I'm either management or labor. There is no walking the tightrope allowed. The employees seek, and deserve as we all do, support, appreciation and fairness. They want answers. They want to make sense out of the conflicting objectives, the unclear, even contradictory guidance. They want security. They want, they expect, me to support them, to defend them, to keep those who threaten the stability of the family at bay. They fix my problems, why can't I fix theirs?

I see their sacrifices. I am with them at midnight, but I also see the employee who sits back waiting for someone to tell him what to do. I see the employee who is sleeping in the truck, but swears he is only resting his eyes. This job would be so much easier if everyone simply concentrated on fixing the broken pipe. The maintenance organizations I've worked with, the ones I've visited around the world, are worlds in and among themselves. Internal conflicts abound, but they look inward for support. Examples of customer service, excellent service, are plentiful but so are acts of complete indifference. Some employees will give 110% (if I can borrow a sporting analogy) all the time, other will run you over on the way to the time clock. Is it my fault an employee waits for someone to give him a job, instead of seeking one out? Am I a Theory X manager? If I weren't such a control freak, if I empowered the employees, would they see the world as I do? If we explain the vision, will they become motivated? Will they not just do management's bidding, but embrace it? Can I expect an employee who can neither read nor write to embrace the information age? Can I really expect an employee who can't pay his bills to embrace Maslow's hierarchy of needs; I'm sorry, self-actualizing doesn't appear to be a viable state. Is this world really different from the ones that embrace empowerment, or are the organizations that proclaim success just like the ones I deal with? Do all organizations have pockets of empowered employees and pockets at the opposite end?

We have decided we must tear down their world and recast it in a way that is acceptable, that meets our needs. We've decided to force it to change, but do we even understand it? The management books tell me it will be difficult, but then give me the five steps needed to do it. No, I cannot accept it! Gordon Graham (1997) presents my ultimate frustration when he states: "In this seemingly endless quest to improve quality, cut costs and increase profitability, we are faced with a paradox: engage the hearts and minds of our employees at the same time we reduce their numbers and increase the workload of those who survive." A paradox: it is more than that, much more.

The consultants, the management books have laid a terrible trip on me. Is it my fault that the employees don't embrace management's objectives? Why can't they see the wisdom of our perspective? As I began this journey I was convinced the solutions were there; I just didn't have the management/leadership ability to make them happen. However, as I continued on this journey, as I began to search other literature, I find that others also question the simple answers. I return to the Hawthorne studies (Roethlisberger, 1939) to re-examine the mythical downfall of Taylor's and my scientific method. I find the significance of these studies was not the surface story that is often highlighted, i.e., that other factors (beyond the physical environment) have an impact on productivity. Instead, the importance of these studies was a development in the understanding of human situations (Roethlisberger, 1939). The studies conclude that for employees the working environment must be looked upon as being permeated with social significance. Brown (1954) argues the most important single factor in determining output is the emotional attitude of the worker toward his work and his workplace. These authors and others reach below the surface issues and call into question some of the assumptions, some of the guiding principles that I so readily accepted over the years. There is a whole new world out there, a world that looks beyond the concrete, a world that asks that more basic questions, a world that looks for understanding. This world complicates my life, but it helps explain it. It also makes me question some of the practices, the tenets that have governed my working life. I've supported the system, I've been a good soldier, I've worked hard; is it time to step off this tightrope?

I've discovered texts that support my contention that a maintenance work force is unique. I've found texts that question the assertion that all we have to do is explain why taking the medicine of increasing productivity is good for us and the workforce will stand in line to take it. We have determined that the maintainer's culture must change to accept our ways, yet we don't understand the glue that holds it together. As I start looking in other directions I find my engineering world, my management training, has done me a disservice. Bolman and Deal (1985) suggest that there is more to leading than we think. Perhaps there is more to facility maintenance than fixing the problem. Perhaps there is more to my being than I think. Have I been looking in the wrong places? My engineering and management texts provided the formulas. I found the answers, but I wasn't asking the right questions. Have we become so focused on the customer that we forgotten the ones in the trenches, the ones doing the work? Does becoming more business-like, does focusing on the big picture, support the objectives, the goals, of the worker? We argue that by giving the employees more influence over the process, by including them in the decision making, by giving them more power, they will become members of the team. They will embrace the objective of our (management's) vision. We suggest that our vision and their vision are one and the same. Is that true?

On the other hand, how does one disagree with management's perspective? It sound right, examples of success can be given, and surely this is what we all are striving for. But is it? We seem to be focusing on those who embrace our objectives. We are saying that those who can't make the transition are going to be left behind. We suggest they will become extinct. In the long run that may be true, but in the short run, in my lifetime, my world has not embraced the evolution, let alone the revolution. The twenty-year carpenter, the groundskeeper, the supervisor promoted on his trades knowledge, not his service perspective, do not have the tools to make the transition. Can the tools be provided? Perhaps in theory, but in reality I need groundskeepers; there will always be groundskeepers, even in the information age.

The members of this world may be decreasing in number but they are not going to become extinct and they see this "new order" as threatening. They see no advantage in being more business-like as their overtime is reduced, their numbers decrease, and the expectation for more work increases. I have trouble convincing the employees that working "smarter," not "harder," should be their goal when their work is measured by physical labor. Smarter equates to more swings of the hammer, not less. The employees' need for trust, for fairness, for security, for more money is understandable; they are legitimate goals. However, do the employees define those terms in the same way I do? I find myself on the fence again, as I did with the customer. I would like to reward the hard workers, the ones I can rely on, but how much money can I give to the one digging the ditch? I would like to assure them that their loyalty to the institution is worth more than being a "little more" productive, but I can't. Our objectives are not the same. I must put my experiences and expectations of my customers, my bosses, and my employees into perspective. Management/leadership is not about formulas, models, or solving problems; it is about balancing. What a complex world in which we work. It defies easy answers, quick solutions. Theories will come and go, we will recreate the solutions over time, but the realities will never change. Yes, there are management/leadership techniques you can learn, yes there is technology that will help you collect data but dealing with people will not allow you to find one shoe fits all. Middle management is, and will remain, a balancing act. You will not, cannot get off the tightrope, your customers, your "employees," the ones on the sidelines telling you how to play the game will always see things differently. There will always be grays, there will always be different perspectives, there will always be unhappy customers, there will always be conflicting objectives, there will always be "inequality," there will always be disgruntled employees, there will always be a lack of communication if you believe better communicating is the answer to all the ills of management. The key to success is how you act and react to in this environment.

Runyon's Law.

"The race is not always to the swift nor the battle to the strong, but that's the way to bet.

-Author Damon Runyon

CHAPTER V
LIVING (SURVIVING) IN THE MIDDLE

"I fired my rifle at the sergeant's command, not daring to open my eyes. I was too scared to look above the wall. They blew Butler's head off. My uniform is drenched in his blood. This is the worst day of my life." But then there is: "My dear, this was one of the finest days of the war. Victory lies within easy reach."

A young corporal penned the first quote. The second comes from a general. Both men were writing about the Battle of Gettysburg, fighting on the same side. This narrative is used by Dr. James Horton to make a point. "The general has the final word. His view becomes history while the other is lost, but both views are valid". The environment in which we work will always consist of conflicting priorities and objectives. Calls for unity, for overarching goals, are fine at the "strategic" level and most will agree with the vision; but, when it comes to dividing up the limited resources one quickly loses the "big picture" perspective. While middle managers seek order, while we strive to make decisions in a quantifiable manner, the environment does not allow for easy answers and measuring one's success is difficult at best. For example, while I do not believe that the value of an employee evaluation system is in its ability to identify the very best, it does allow us to convince ourselves and others that we have an objective measure of performance. Similarly, as we develop systems to account for every expenditure, we can say we are more efficient, as long as we do not calculate how much it costs to collect the data that allows us to "feel and look good." I hearken back to my old commander: "If the grass is cut, if the buildings are painted, if the guard at the gate looks sharp, we look like we know what we're doing." We may look good, but the whitewash could be holding up a false front. But is that important?

As I reflect on my experiences and seek to understand the relationships that influence the "day to day" activities, I realize that the work world will not and cannot be a sea of tranquility. I cannot "will" away, assume away, or manage or lead away the conflicting priorities, the unclear objectives, the political decisions, the limited resources, or the many problems these realities bring with them. It is our job to balance them. It is a lonely job, an all-consuming job, a job that demands total commitment, and a job that requires a long-range view but a short-range focus.

Argyis (1975) suggests that managers/leaders try hard to be client-centered, employee-centered, group-centered, subordinate-centered, person-centered as well as organizationally-centered, production-centered, superior-centered, decision-centered, and task-centered. He concludes, since real life is multi-dimensional, one has to be reality-centered and accept that there is no predetermined set of best ways, and that a manager has to diagnose what is reality.

Similarly, Sjöstrand (1997) uses the metaphor of Janus, a Roman god, to describe this need to have multiple faces. Janus was associated with entries, transits, and exits and had a double face, allowing the god to look simultaneously in different, in fact opposite directions. It was this ability that allowed him to function in a world of ambiguity, where he had to look upward in the hierarchy to face principals, stake holders, owners, and customers, and downward to face employees. Janusian thinking implies that managers should not use all their energy in trying to eliminate contradictory ingredients or dissonant parts, but rather recognize that these conflicting entities will never disappear.

Sjöstrand also notes that to influence the activities performed by other people, all of them quite different from one another and with different ambitions and reasons for participating, is certainly a difficult, if not impossible, task. Perhaps at best, he continues, managers can hope to help modify a state of organized chaos and produce something that can be described as semi-coordinated. Bureaucracies surely fit this description, for on the surface, chaos seems to reign supreme. That is not a condemnation and I'm not suggesting that it is a bad thing, even though the word "bureaucracy," like politics, has become synonymous with everything we don't like. In reality, they are both legitimate methods of assessing and dealing with our complex world. A bureaucracy is nothing more than a social invention which relies on rules, reason, and law to influence events and allocate resources, while politics uses the power of negotiation and compromise to do the same thing (Bennis, 1970). Like any process, there are inherent benefits and problems associated with each, and while criticism of either system may highlight the problems each have it fails to provide solutions. Nonetheless, the inherent difficulties should be comforting to those who believe they should have all the answers. I take solace in some of the literature that doesn't support the "how to" books. Some of the most quoted names in the literature lend some support to my perspective. Maslow suggests: "The boss is really not one of the boys, he cannot be expressive and open about his own thoughts and anxieties as others are permitted and encouraged to be. A successful boss must have the power and ability to keep his mouth shut, not to depress or upset the morale of the workers." (Bennis, 1970, p. 35) Some may disagree with that assertion, but to me it is comforting. Meanwhile, Gomberg (1966) goes further and says managerial behavior is dictated by the nature of technology and the economic constraints of limited available resources. He argues that someone has to assume responsibility for the ultimate decisions, and others are bound to be frustrated by that decision. While these statements make me feel better, the authors still qualify their remarks and even Maslow waffles when he states his concerns are not a rejection of what human relations theory has to say about management. That the facts do support participative management when the culture is amenable, when people are psychologically healthy, and when general conditions are good--that perfect world again.

I can't sit back, smug in my knowledge that there isn't a solution that everyone agrees with, for I must fix the heat and meet the needs of customers and my bosses. There will be changes; there have to be changes. Yet some of this change is very disconcerting. Bennis (1970) describes the demise of bureaucracy and mentions, as an aside, that manual laborers, the less educated, those who desire to work under conditions of high authority may find their jobs disappearing, while others will be automated. Disappear or be automated, what's the difference? His aside is a large part of my world. Bennis concludes that change, technology, humanistic management, adaptive problem solving, temporary systems of diverse specialists, and flux will govern the business world of the future [now]. Even the most vocal critics of change must acknowledge change is constant. As the customers and employees I talk to reflect on their past, it is obvious that we all have seen tremendous change over the years. Practices, behavior, and procedures that were acceptable in the past are no longer acceptable, and in most cases the change was accepted without tremendous upheaval. That is not to say that all went willingly, that there were not, are not, lapses of attention. Pin-ups in a locker can still be found every once in a while. A smoker can be found in a building every once in a while. The old school raises its head occasionally, but gradual change is evident if one stops and looks. That may be the key. Change is gradual; change is incremental and establishing common objectives and consequently shared strategies is a strenuous task, and ambitions have to be rather modest (Sjöstrand, 1997)

I almost convinced myself that the advocates of change are right, but then I'm reminded--the more things change, the more they stay the same. Is that being negative? Am I fulfilling the self-fulfilling prophecy (Herzburg, 1967)? I am doubting myself again, but I remind myself the issues don't change. I've dealt with personnel problems for thirty-five years: productivity (the lack thereof) was a problem years ago; walls have been built without considering the HVAC for a long time; short term objectives frequently overshadow the long term strategy; and proposed fixes for funding shortages never seem to work. We change a lot but the issues remain.

The frustration for one who wants to solve the problem and move on is great, but we need to quit whining, quit complaining, and accept the reality. Sound advice, can I practice what I preach? Arygis' (1957) interview with several foremen says it better than I ever could; there are some things that never change. The foreman concludes:

> I'll tell you one thing that you can put down in your little black book and I want you to remember this and that is that the supervisor is a "bumping post!" That is something you can remember, he is a "bumping post!" because he is in the middle. He has to take it from ends; and those running the place don't give him any credit for it. It is like being between the devil and the deep blue sea.

If I accept this reality how do I deal with my internal struggle? My frustration with management theories, with mathematical models, and with efforts to quantify the art of leadership has not lessened. If anything, it grows with my changing perspective. Management and leadership are not mathematical models. They are not a list of personal characteristics. They are not cookbooks. We can continue to look for a panacea that will take away the conflict, that will ensure productivity, efficiency, and effectiveness, and will allow everyone to see the wisdom of the "system's" solution; but, while we can influence, while we can change emphasis, we cannot eliminate the underlying issues. A pessimistic attitude? No. It is a reality that reflects the rationality of conflicting goals, objectives, and agendas. A rationality that is neither a purely subjective phenomenon, nor an objective universal quality as stressed in most modern logic. It is a social construction, and inter-subjective phenomenon specific to certain periods as well as to particular cultures. Rationality simultaneously represents the outcome of interactions and is produced by them (Sjöstrand, 1997). Sjöstrand continues that the dividing line between what is rational and what is irrational is hard both to define and to describe, and that it is continuously being exceeded and crossed, but at the same time being re-established and re-enforced. It is a borderline--diffuse, floating, and shifting.

Significant emotional events (Massey, 1979), one's frame of reference (Bolman & Deal, 1984), one paradigm (Kuhn, 1962), one's approach to decision-making (Allison, 1971), one's make-up or personality (Keirsey & Bates, 1984), one's environment, and perhaps one's age, all influences one's view of the world. With those myriad of factors bombarding you and ones around you, is it any wonder there are no answers, only more questions and a tightrope to walk? I cannot accept the rhetoric, the argument, that all that is needed to solve our management problems is to empower the employee, to improve supervision, to focus on a vision statement, to establish long term goals, to plan, to facilitate, to coach, etc., etc.. All those ideas have some merit, but conflicts will remain. One has to realize the limited resources, the various perspectives, the focus on what people can visualize (the grass, not a multi-million dollar electrical project), and the fact our product touches everyone leads to conflicts. That fact is reality; it must be acknowledged, and that's the way it will always be. As decisions are made, as resources are allocated, there is seldom consensus. There may be acceptance but that does not mean anyone abandons his/her cause or accepts that the final word has been said. The right solution is determined by one's perspective. The problem is solved only if the solution meets your objectives. Hence, the manager is confronted with a paradox: irrational actions are sometimes rational and rational actions are sometimes irrational (Sjöstrand, 1997). This realization certainly puts strain on my approach to the world.

Huston Smith (1997) during a speech at the Smithsonian Institute, describes the "post modern" (post scientific method) period as one in which the shortcoming of our reliance on science to solve every problem is recognized. I have come, belatedly, to understand that movement. While we owe much to science, we now expect too much from it, and are trying to force it to solve problems that defy a mathematical solution. The scientific method is powerful, but it is limited. Smith proposed that we have the most difficulty when trying to explain the following scientifically: values (we can measure what people like, but cannot measure what they should like); meaning (we can deal with cognitive issues, but not existential); purpose (we can measure behavior, but not teleology); quality (what does whiteness (in my business, "clean") mean to different individuals?); things that are invisible or immaterial; and finally, we cannot explain superiority (we can measure skills, but not questions of intellect). Yet, in all these areas we are trying to convince ourselves, and even worse, others that we have the ability to quantify those concepts. We judge people on the quality of their customer service, but against what standard? What variables must we control? Yes, there are degrees of quality; yes, we "know" quality when we see it, but if someone's paycheck (someone who can't pay his bills) is determined by our understanding of the quality of his work, you can bet our objectivity will be questioned. Our objective measures of the world run headlong into our subjective understanding.

We must move beyond the technical frame of reference. That is not where the decisions will be made. A facility engineer's training does him/her a disservice as we move to "management/leadership." My one course in philosophy (logic) did not to help me understand the complexities I now deal with. My twenty hours in statistics have long since left my day-to-day needs. It has taken a lot of years, a lot of experience, a lot of pain to reach this point. This move to understanding is what is required to be successful. It is this reality that the "management" courses need to stress, for as Sjöstrand (1997) notes: "the dualism between the rational and irrational in management theory and practice is a consequence of the fact that major parts of the management science have been founded on normative idealistic theories rather than on theories relating to empirical studies of actual managerial practices."

I reflect back on my military summer camp and all the emphasis on rolling up my socks, on bouncing quarters off a properly made bed, on the proper way to squeeze the toothpaste. I saw these as stupid things, things that had no place in this engineer's view of the world. As I complained bitterly to my training instructor (after I received my commission), his response stopped me in my tracks. "I know they are stupid but we have to create a stress-filled environment if we are to assess your ability to handle it. Our approach is not ideal, and if you can think of a better one, let me know." Over the years I've failed to find a better test and unfortunately I have also failed to handle the stress on a number of occasions. I have grown tired of hitting my head against a brick wall, but maybe I need to step back and ask why am I doing it? "Perhaps we've lost our way when we forget that the heart of leadership lies in the hearts of leaders. We fooled ourselves thinking that sheer bravado or sophisticated analysis techniques could respond to our deepest concerns" (Bolman & Deal). As I begin to accept that reality several key "truths" begin to come into focus. The first is summarized by a "one pager" that captures the difference between a boss and a leader. A choice that we can all make and one that I believe is fundamental if you want to be a successful middle manager. However, as always, there is a caution, it is not an either or proposition. There are times when you have to be a boss, the person that says this is the way it is going to be, but even then, the success of that approach is often determined by your long term approach, i.e., if your employees are used to being led by you, when you have to be the boss their commitment will most likely be stronger than if you always dictate. Perhaps the old adage, you can lead a horse to water but you can't make him drink, is a good analogy. A boss can dictate, the employee will most likely "follow directions" but their commitment, their willingness to take up the challenge will be predicated on how they feel about you.

Being a leader consists of more than having the position, more than having the power over others; instead, it requires that people know you, believe in you, and understand that you appreciate what they are doing. Pretty difficult concept to grasp, even more difficult to quantify...you can learn techniques to be a leader but there is some truth in the old axiom, "Leaders are born. Not made," because:

- A boss says I, a leader says we

- A boss takes credit, a leader give credit

- A boss commands, a leader asks

- A boss says go, a leader says let's go

- A boss places blame, a leader fixes the problem

- A boss builds himself and his unit up by tearing other units down,

- A leader does not tear other units down

Even though I see myself in the "leadership" camp, I must admit, I must realize, being the "boss" has its moments. This balancing act is tough. This complexity, this need to have a split personality is very, very difficult. The second truth is highlighted by Briskin (1996) when he notes: "In the workplace we have become polarized between managing the outer organization – work pressures, organizational objectives, managerial structure and the inner organization of people – emotional attitudes, mental processes, cooperative spirit. The challenge is to build a bridge between the world of personal, subjective and even unconscious elements of individual experiences and the world of organizations that demand rationality, efficiency, and personal sacrifices."

This concept of polarity is not new, it has been around for decades, if not centuries, but the application to the world of management is gaining renewed interest. As I reflect on Brisken's work, on Rittel's and Webber's wicked problems, on Sjostrond's work, there is the realization that many, if not most, of the issues middle managers deal with do not fit the model for each x, there is one, and only one, y. This reality, the realization that my scientific model does not work, was, for me, what Massy would call a "significant emotional event." An event that has such an impact that it changes one's "world view." I have found that many of the problems experienced by middle managers are, by default, the result of polarities such as:

- Providing direction vs. inviting participation

- My department vs. the whole organization

- Short term vs. long term goals and objectives

- Give freedom vs. hold responsible

- Manage vs. lead

- Customer service vs. customer servant

Many of these issues faced in the work place, as well as outside the work place, are polarities to manage, not problems to solve. The organization that I am currently working for, and the last that I will work for in the capacity of a middle manager; is wrestling with building a senior team of directors from 5 different departments that have different roles, different measures of success, different needs, different responsibilities. The vision is to place the needs of the "senior team" above those of the individual departments. While I have some real reservations, as described throughout this book, one interesting reality was brought to the group by the consultants who were hired to help us place "group" needs, above departmental needs, "Plurality Management."

As one explores this concept of polarity, you can soon get far afield from the world of management. The American Polarity Theory Association argues that energy fields and currents exist everywhere in nature, an argument that this engineer will readily accept; however, to jump to the conclusion, or accept the premise, that a proper balance is the key to good health, a good life, an understanding of universe, is more than I can grasp at this time and a subject for a whole other conversation. Further, I caution us not to believe that embracing this "new" theory, this revelation, or assure a better organization, will guarantee the achievement of one's goals, will solve conflicts, will be the answer to your problems. In fact, I believe understanding these polarities, acknowledging your need to focus on both poles, accepting the fact the pendulum will swing one way, and then the other, only complicates our life. The theorists will argue you need to maximize the "upside" of both poles, in that way you will have a win-win. I'm sorry, that sound good, but it is not the reality. Instead, I will argue knowledge of polarities simply means you will always be on that tread mill. The tightrope always requires constant balancing. An article on polarity management – (note the word <u>management</u>) concludes:

> "Those managers, parents, teachers, government leaders, teams, organizations, and nations that develop the ability to distinguish between solvable problems and unsolvable polarities and have the ability to respond effectively to each will out-perform those who can't distinguish between them and who try to address all issues from a problem solving perspective."

I'm not sure how you measure "out performs," in fact, even saying you can measure the outcome of polarity management is questionable, but that is not important. Instead we need to think about this reality. "To recognize the simultaneous presence of both rational and the irrational in the practice of life is an important achievement, but to accept the rationality of the irrational and vice versa represents an even more dramatic step" (Sjöstrand, 1997, p. 197). What a simple statement. What a powerful realization. What may appear non-rational, or even worse, irrational, to me may make perfect sense to those who are viewing the same picture from a different perspective, from a different frame of reference. If I can see the other's viewpoint, the other's underlying perspective, there may be room for understanding and there may be a way to move beyond a particular path.

Briskin (1996) describes a manager who was so confident of his intellectual skills of figuring out and fixing problems that he had never perceived a need to plunge into the murky and shifting recesses of his own mind. How did he know me? I'm not sure I am sold with my intellect but I am certainly focused on fixing problems. I am a fixer; that is what I am supposed to be. Am I prepared to be anything else? Vaill (1989) suggests that a modern leader-manager is required to be able to reflect and philosophize to a degree that sometimes astonishes (and infuriates) the down-to-earth, no-nonsense, let's-get-on-with-it sort of men and women who have traditionally held those jobs. That is getting pretty personal. Oates (1971) describes me when he talks about workaholics and society's enabling effort. He says I have no value that is not subordinated to the good of the organization, that I do not work to a certain set of hours; that I am always on call. That isn't a suggestion of long hours, but it is in fact an assessment of one who is always working, even when supposedly relaxing. As I read through the article, it stared back at me; it was all encompassing. I must be in control. I must solve. My job and my being feed on each other, support each other.

I watch with fascination as the District of Columbia Public Schools contend with a decaying infrastructure, deferred maintenance, inadequate funding. This is the University of Massachusetts' scenario with a slightly different twist. The public schools are reorganized. A new leader is hired, but in addition to having to manage their way out of their problems they are forced to commit resources. But even that step causes conflict. Everyone agrees the work must be done, but they can't agree on how. When challenged by a judge overseeing the efforts, the new superintendent remarks... "I don't feel that I have to ask about doing my job. It is against my nature; my inner everything to ask permission to do something, which I know is my responsibility" (Washington Post, Oct. 26, 1997, p. B1). When asked why he authorized work "without permission" the Superintendent said, "I would rather go ahead and do something and find out later we could, then ask and find out earlier we can't." My kind of guy; Julius Becton, a retired Army general. Is it a "military" mind set? I don't think so. Perhaps those with this mind set gravitate to the military, but the military doesn't have a monopoly on the behavior. There are many who need to challenge the:

> For men are prone to go it blind
> Along the calf-paths of the mind
> And work away from sun to sun
> To do what other men have done...
> Calf's Path

But even the acknowledgement that my yes/no view of the world does not work, I still have to deal with the conflicts I live with on my three levels of existence. The surface where things get done and you have to put on your many masks, below the surface where you have to struggle to find the right, the appropriate, the "correct" method, theory, model, practice, technique, that allows you to navigate the surface, and then the internal struggles of balancing your work life, with your life. But then, I have to accept, you need to accept, the reality that there is no answer. You need to manage the interactions, the interfaces. So what can we take away from this journey, this exploration? What are the gold nuggets, the themes that emerge from our travels? How can you stay balanced, let alone make progress? We need to accept there is nothing but constant questioning. You must find peace in that reality. Vaill (1989) said of his book, "Managing as a Performing Art," that it could perform no higher service than to stimulate readers to critique the ideas he presents, to play with them, to turn them around, and sometimes to work hard to puncture them. I can only hope my story can do the same.

I wouldn't be true to myself if I professed to have some new method to guarantee success, for there are literally thousands of books, thousands of experts who have given advice to those walking my path. Perhaps it is nothing more than what I believe is the major benefit of going to conferences, to hearing motivational speeches, of being exposed to and talking to others in the same boat. You find out that you are not alone. The problems you face are not unique. The individuals sitting on either side of you have their stories, their experiences, and they are not unlike your own. In fact, you find that you shouldn't be beating up on yourself quite as much as you are. Walker (1979), in his book, The Effective Administrator, provides a shopping list of things that a manager should do. At first I discarded them in a huff. They were common sense; they were techniques. They were little things. They were nothing new.

But in hindsight, he was right -- being effective is not mastering some management theory that will guarantee success; it does, however, require the ability to be a bridge between two worlds, to be willing to accept responsibility, to be willing to fight the status quo and to thank people every day. In addition, one must understand that he is not going to make everyone happy, and that it is OK to be frustrated. It is OK to walk the tightrope. It is OK, in fact it should be mandatory, to find some relief from the constant need to balance. It is also important to listen and not be so quick to solve. For those like me, that is no doubt the hardest lesson of all. Above all, one must learn to balance in all areas, above, below, and internally.

My recommendations are not profound. There is nothing revolutionary--I have no new management theory. Perhaps the salvation is in the simplicity. So easy, yet so hard; it is a constant journey. In order to survive (that is at least one definition of success) you need to:

1) Accept the fact that you are in a political world, regardless of your job. That those political issues all have to be addressed, but cannot be solved. Common objectives do not translate into everyone agreeing on a course of action. You have to be an arbitrator, a politician, a person who cannot allow agendas to get in the way of solving the problem. Make a decision, do what is best for the organization, and expect complaints.

2) Support and praise your people. This should be obvious, and is certainly in most, if not all the how to books. Unfortunately, few do it. If you do not say "thank you" every day you are making a mistake. However, make sure it is honest, make sure the person knows you are sincere but don't be surprised if they want you to do something for them. A slippery slope, but one you better be on.

3) Challenge the status quo. You have to be willing to go out on the limb (yes it may be cut off). I love the suggestion of simply not answering the phone, or the email (especially if it is from higher headquarters) every once and awhile, just to see if anyone is really interested. Again a dangerous place to be and you have to pick your poison, but it's fun. Seriously, there is a fine art in knowing when to push the envelope, fall on your sword, whatever you want to call it, but be willing to do it.

4) Think long-term but live day-to-day. Ok, I don't follow my own advice here. While I appreciate the long term, while I understand the vision, I don't spend much time thinking about it. The day to day is where it's at! You have to know what's going on; you have to focus on today. That is success.

5) Be customer-oriented but support your people. This is tough. You are on a fine line you have to know when are you making excuses or when are you supporting your people. You have to avoid the first, do the second.

6) Do as I say, not as I do. Have a life beyond the job. So easy to say, so hard to do, but a key to your ability to survive.

7) Understand you will always be on that tightrope; you will always be moving through the quadrants of the polarities of your work life.

8) And most importantly, accept the fact that you are the one who makes it happen, you are the one who translates the vision to "getting things done." You will be challenged, you will be chastised, but when the chips are on the line they will rely on you to get it done. It is the work we do. I learned late,

and I'm still trying to learn that middle management, maybe all jobs, requires a balancing act.

None of these statements are new; as I've noted, there really isn't anything new in management. These suggestions are in all the how-to books. The doing takes practice, you need to do it every day and accept the fact that it doesn't work all the time. But keep trying. There is nothing revolutionary about middle management but it can be evolutionary and perhaps if we understand each other's view of the world, perhaps that hand-painted sign can be changed to read:

WHAT IF THE UNDERSTANDING YOU GAIN
CHANGES WHAT YOU BELIEVE, AND CREATES A NEW
REALITY?

And what if that reality allows you to balance your work life with your personal life...if you can do that, you win...

REFERENCES

Adams, S. (1996). The <u>Dilbert principle.</u> New York: Harper Collins.

Ahumada, M. M. (1993). An analysis of state for budgeting in higher education. In D. W. Breneman, L. L. Leslie, & R. E. Anderson (Eds), <u>Finance in higher education,</u> (pp. 331-354). Needham Heights, M.A: Ashe Reader Series, Ginn.

Allen, R., & Chaffee, E. E. (1981). <u>Management fads in higher education.</u> Unpublished manuscript, National Center for Higher Education Management Systems, Inc. Boulder, CO.

Allison, G. T. (1971). <u>Essence of decision: Explaining the Cuban missile crisis.</u> Boston: Harper Collins.

Alvesson, M. (1993). <u>Cultural perspectives on organizations.</u> Chippenham, Wiltshire, Great Britain: Cambridge University Press.

Anthony, R. N. (1977, April 27). Zero-based budgeting is a fraud. <u>Wall Street Journal,</u> pp. Al, A4.

Aoki, T (1991). <u>Teaching and in-dwelling between two curriculum worlds.</u> Edmonton, Alberta: University of Alberta.

REFERENCES

Argyris, C. (1957). <u>Personality and organization.</u> New York: Harper & Row.

Austin, J. T., & Klein, H. J. (1996). Work motivation and goal striving. In. K. R. Murphy (Ed), <u>Individual differences and behavior in organizations,</u> (pp. 209-293). San Francisco: Jossey-Bass.

Badia, P., & Runyon, R. P. (1982). <u>Fundamentals of behavioral research.</u> Reading, MA: Addison-Wesley.

Bailey, S. K. (1978). The peculiar mixture: Public norms and private space. In W. C. Hobbs (Ed), <u>Government regulation of higher education</u> (pp. 103-111). Cambridge, MA: Ballenger.

Bailey, S. K. (1993, October). <u>Education and the state.</u> Keynote address of the American Council on Education, at the 56th Annual Meeting, Washington, DC.

Baldridge, V. J. (1971). <u>Acadenuc governance: Research on institutional politics and decision-making.</u> Berkely, CA: McCutcheon

Baldridge, V. J., Curtis, D. V., Eshker, G. P., & Riley, G. L. (1991). Alternative models of governance in higher education. In M. W. Peterson, E.E. Chaffee, & T. H. White (Eds.), <u>Organization and governance in higher education</u> (4th ed., pp. 30-45). Needham Heights, MA: Ashe Reader Series, Ginn.

Becton, J. W. (1977, October 26). Contest of will contributes to chaos at D. C. schools. <u>Washington Post.</u> P. B1.

Bennis, W. (1970). Beyond bureaucracy. In W. Bennis (Ed.), <u>American bureaucracy</u> (pp. 3-16). New Brunswick, NY: Transaction Books.

Benveniste, G. (1989). Mastering the politics of planning. San Franciso: Jossey-Bass.

Berkley, G. E. (1984). The craft of public administration. Newton, MA: Allyn & Bacon.

Berman, L. M., Hultgren, F. H., Lee, D., Rivkin, M. S., & Roderick, J. A. (1991). Toward curriculum for being. Albany: State University of New York.

Bilello, J. (1993). Deciding to build: University organization and the design of academic buildings. Unpublished doctoral dissertation, University of Maryland, College Park.

Birnbaum, R. (1988). How colleges work. San Francisco: Jossey-Bass

Briskin, A. (1996). The stirring of soul in the workplace. San Francisco: Jossey-Bass

Blake, R. B., & Mouton, H. S. (1978). Grid organization development. In W. W. Natemeyer (Ed.), Classics of organizational behavior (pp. 328-335). Oak Park, IL: Moore.

Bok, D. (1982). Beyond the ivory tower: Social responsibilities of the modern university. Boston: Harvard University Press.

Bolman, L. G., & Deal, T. E. (1984). Modern approaches to understanding and managing organizations. San Francisco: Jossey-Bass

Bolman, L. G., & Deal, T. E. (1985). Leading with soul. San Fracisco: Jossey-Bass.

REFERENCES

Breneman, D. W. (1993). <u>Higher education: On a collision course with new realities.</u> The AGB Occasional Paper Series, Washington, DC.

Brown, J. A. C. (1954). <u>The social psychology of industry.</u> Baltimore: Penguin.

Canning, C. (1992). Interpretive inquiry: If you are going to use it, you will be doing it. In N. Heggerson & A. Bowman (Eds.), <u>Forming educational policy and practice through interpretive inquiry</u> (pp. 61-81). Lancaster, PA: Technomic.

Carr, W., & Kemmis, S. (1986). <u>Becoming critical.</u> London and Philadelphia: Palmer.

Chaffee, E. E. (1983). <u>Rational decision making in higher education.</u> Boulder, CO: National Center for Higher Education Management.

Chafee, E. E. (1991). The role of rationality in university budgeting. In M. W. Peterson (Ed.), <u>Organization and governance in higher education</u> (4th ed., pp. 253-267). Needham Heights, MA: Ashe Reader Series, Ginn.

Choate, P., & Walters, S. (1981). <u>America in ruins: Beyond the public works pork barrel.</u> Washington, DC: Council of State Planning Agencies.

Churchman, C. W. (1971). <u>The design of inquiring systems: Basic concepts of systems and organizations.</u> New York: Basic Books

Collinson, D. L. (1988). Engineering humor: Masculinity, joking and conflict in shop floor relations. <u>Organization Studies, 12,</u> 181-199.

Critical capital needs. (1995, Fall). A Report to the Regents, Office of the Vice President for Policy and Planning, Office of the Executive Vice President, University of Maryland, College Park, MD.

Cuff, D. (1991). Architecture: The story of practice. Cambridge, MA: The MIT Press, pp. 81-91.

Culbert, S. A. & McDonough, J. J. (1985). Radical management, New York: The Free Press.

Daigneau, W. (1997). Product based management. Facilities management, APPA Sept/Oct. 1997, 13 (5), 43-47.

Dill, D. D. (1991). The management of academic culture: Notes on the management of meaning and social integration. In M. W. Peterson (Ed.), Organization and governance in higher education. (4th ed., pp. 182-194). Needham Heights, MA: Ashe Reader Series, Ginn.

Dill, D. D. (1991). The nature of administrative behavior in higher education. In M.W. Peterson (Ed.), Organization and governance in higher education. (4th ed.) (pp. 369-388). Needham Heights, MA: Ashe Reader Series, Ginn.

Dillon, R. O. (1986). Facilities management (2nd ed.). Alexandria, VA: Association of Physical Plant Administrators of Universities and Colleges.

Dilthey, W. (1969). Dilthey: Hermeneutics as foundation of the Geisteswissenschaften. In R. E. Palmer, Hermeneutics. Evanston, IL: Northwestern University.

Dow, R. (1997). Insights from a customer enthusiast. <u>Facilities manager.</u> Nov/Dec., 1997, 13 (6), 21-32.

Dreyfus, H. (1994). <u>Being-in-the –world.</u> Cambridge, MA: MIT press.

Drucker, P. F. (1974). <u>Management: Tasks responsibilities practices.</u> New York: Harper & Row.

Dunn, J. A. (1989). <u>Financial planning guidelines for facility renewal and adaption.</u> Ann Arbor, MI: the Society for College and University Planning.

Eisenhardt, K. M., & Zbrackie, M. J. (1992). Strategic decision making. <u>Strategic Management Journal,</u> 13, 17-37.

Etzioni, A. (1986). Rationality is anti-entropic. <u>Journal of Economic Psychology,</u> 2, 17-36.

<u>Facilities stewardship in the 1990's.</u> Proceedings of the First Institute for Facilities Finance in Higher Education (1990, Nov.). Alexandria, VA: Association of Physical Plant Administrators of Universities and Colleges.

Fairholm, G. W. (1994). <u>Leadership and the culture of trust.</u> Westport, CT: Praeger Publishers.

Friedland, E. I. (1974). <u>Introduction to the concept of rationality in political science</u> (pp. 1-26). Morristown, NJ: General Learning Press.

Gardner, J. W. (1990). <u>On leadership.</u> New York: The Free Press.

Gomberg, W. (1966). The trouble with democratic management. In W. Bennis (Ed.), American bureaucracy (pp. 39-52). Managing change in the workplace. Facilities Engineering. May/June 1997, pp. 22-26.

Graham, G. (1997, May/June). Managing change in the workplace. Facilities Engineering. May/June 1997, pp. 22-26.

Graves, C. W. (1970). Levels of existence: An open system theory of value. Journal of Humanistic Psychology, 10 (2), pp. 131-155.

Green, P. P. (1994). If your heart is in your dreams...A phenomenological view of the principalship. Unpublished dissertation, University of Maryland, College Park.

Haggans, M. (1995, Summer). Fire the architect! The conflicting perspectives of architects & facilities managers. Facilities Manager, pp. 41-43.

Harvey, J. B. (1988). The Abilene paradox and other meditations n management. Lexington, MA: Lexington Books.

Harvey, J. B. (1989, May/Jun). Trust and organizational effectiveness. Technology Review, pp. 271-277.

Heidegger, M. (1971). Building dwelling thinking. (Albert Hofstadter, Trans.). New York: Harper and Row.

Heidegger, M. (1977). The questions concerning technology and other essays. (W. Lovett, Trans.). New York: Harper and Row.

Heller, J. (1961). Catch 22. New York: Dell.

Hellman, B. (1995, Summer). Partnering: a midterm report card, Facilities Manager, pp. 33-35.

Herzberg, F. (1967, Jan-Feb). One more time: How do you motivate employees, Classics of Organizational Behavior (pp. 95-106).

Hoffer, F. (1969). Working and thinking on the waterfront. New York: Harper & Row.

Horton, J. (1977, March 27). In George Washington University advertisement. Washington Post. P. B24.

Janis, I. K. (1971). Groupthink. In W. E. Natemeyer (Ed.), Classics of organizational behavior (pp. 156-164). Oak Park, IL: Moore.

Kaiser, H. H. (1993). The facilities audit. Monograph published by Association of Physical Plant Administrators of Colleges and Universities. Alexandria, VA/

Keirsey, D., & Bates, M. (1984). Please understand me. (5th ed.). Del Mar, CA: Prometheus, Nemesis.

Koontz, H. (1978). The management theory jungle. In W. E. Natemeyer (Ed.), Classics of organizational behavior. (pp. 10-30). Oak Park, IL: Moore.

Kotter, J. P. (1990). A force for change. New York: The Free Press. Kromkowski, J. (1995). Report on supervision and work life for the department of physical plant. Unpublished manuscript, University of Maryland at College Park.

Kruger, D. (1981). An introduction to phenomenological psychology. Pittsburgh, PA: Duquesne University.

Kuhn, T. S. (1962). The structure of scientific revolutions. Chicago: University of Chicago.

Landau, M. (1969). Redundancy, rationality, and the problem of duplication and overlap. Public Administrative Review. xxix, (4), 346-358

Layzell, D. T., & Lyddon, J. W. (1993). Budgeting for higher education at the state level: Enigma, paradox, and ritual. In D. W. Breneman, L. L. Leslie, & R. E. Anderson (Eds.), Finance in higher education. (pp. 311-330). Needham Heights, MA: Ashe Reader Series, Ginn.

Lee. D. (1991). To be in a world of wicked problems. In L. M. Berman, F. H. Hulgren, D. Lee, M. S. Rivkin, & J. A. Roderick (Eds.), Toward curriculum for being. (pp. 116-121). State University of New York: Albany.

Lindblom, C. E. (1959). The science of muddling through. The Journal of the American Society of Public Administration, xix, (2) 79-88.

Luthans, F. (1977). Contemporary readings in organizational behavior. (2nd ed.). New York: McGraw-Hill.

Mannheim. (1940). Man and society in an age of reconstruction. London: Rutledge and Kegan Paul, Ltd.

Martel, L. (1986). Mastering change. New York: Simon and Schuster.

Marston, W. (1928). The emotions of normal people. London: Harcourt, Bruce & Co.

Martin, J., & Meyerson D. (1988). Organizational cultures and denial, channeling and acknowledgement of ambiguity. In L. R.

Pondy, R. J. Boland, Jr. & H. Thomas (Eds.), Managing <u>ambiguity and change</u> (pp. 132-155) New York: Wiley.

Maslow, A. H. (1964). The superior person. In W. G. Bennis (Ed.), <u>American bureaucracy</u> (pp. 27-38). New Brunswick, NY: Transaction Books.

Maslow, A. H. (1978). A theory of human motivation. In W. E. Natemeyer (Ed.), <u>Classics of organizational behavior</u> (pp. 42-57). Oak Park, IL: Moore.

Massey, M. (1979). <u>The people puzzle.</u> Reston, VA: Reston Publishing Co., Inc., of Prentice Hall.

McDaniel, S. P. (1984). <u>Formula application for renewal and replacement of educational facilities.</u> Unpublished doctoral dissertation, University of Missouri-Columbia.

McFadden, R. D. (1976). Audit of an Audit. In R. J. Furst, V . F. Mitchell, & W. R. Nord (Eds.), <u>Organizational reality</u> (pp. 393-395). Santa Monica, CA: Goodyear Publishing.

McGregor, D. M. (1978). The human side of enterprise. In W. E. Natemeyer (Ed.), <u>Classics of organizational behavior</u> (pp. 12-18). Oak Park, IL: Moore.

Meisinger, R. J., Jr. (1989). Introduction to special issue on the relationship between planning and budgeting. <u>Planning for Higher Education, 2,</u> (4), 111-117. Society for College and University Planning.

Meisinger, R. J., Jr. (1994). <u>College and university budgeting,</u> (2nd ed). Washington, DC: National Association of College and University Business Officers.

Mintzberg, H. (1979). The structuring of organizations. New Jersey: Prentice-Hall.

Mintzberg, H. (1991). The professional bureaucracy. In M. W. Peterson (Ed.), Organization and governance in higher education, (4th ed., pp. 53-75). Needham Heights, MA: Ashe Reader Series, Ginn Press.

Mintzberg, H. (1994). The rise and fall of strategic planning. New York: The Free Press.

Mooney, R. (1975). The researcher himself. In W. Pinar (Ed.) Curriculum theorizing: The reconceptualists (pp. 175-207). Berkeley, CA: McCutcheon.

Moustakas, C. (1994). Phenomenological research methods. London: Sage.

Oates, W. (1971). Confessions of a workaholic: the facts about work addiction. New York: World Publishing.

Ouchi, W. (1981). Theory Z: How American business can meet the Japanese challenge. Reading, MA: Addison Wesley.

Ouchi, W. G., & Wilkins, A. L. (1985). Organizational culture. Annual Review of Sociology, II. 457-83.

Palmer, R. E. (1969). Hermeneutics. Evanston, IL: Northwestern University Press.

Peter, L. J., & Hull, R. (1970). The Peter principle. New York: Bantam.

Peters, T., & Austin, N. (1985). A passion for excellence. New York: Random House.

Peterson, V. (1996). Combating age and stereotypes. <u>Facilities Manager,</u> Oct. 96, <u>12</u> (4), 13.

Piantanida, M. (1992). Interpretive inquiry: Implications for professional education. In N. Haggerson & A. Bowman (Eds.), <u>Informing educational policy and practice through interpretive inquiry</u> (pp. 39-59). Lancaster, PA: Technomic.

Pirsig, R. W. (1974). <u>Zen and the art of motorcycle maintenance.</u> New York: Bantam.

Reynolds, G. <u>Building quality,</u> as cited in Daigneau, W. (1997), Product based management. <u>Facilities Manager,</u> Sept/Oct. 97, <u>13</u> (5), 43-47.

Risser, J. (1997). Hermeneutics and the voice of the other. Albany, NY: State University of New York Press.

Rittel, H. W. J., & Webber, M. M. (1973). Dilemmas in a general theory of planning. <u>Policy Sciences 4:</u> pp. 155-69.

Roberts, W. (1985). <u>Leadership secrets of atella the hun.</u> New York: Warner Books.

Roethlisberger, F. J., & Dickson, W. T. (1939). <u>Management and the worker.</u> Harvard University: Cambridge, MA.

Rosenzweig, R. M., with Turlington, B. (1982). <u>The research universities and their patrons.</u> Berkeley: University of California Press.

Rush, S. C., & Johnson, S. J. (1989). <u>The decaying American campus: A ticking time bomb.</u> A joint report of APPA and NACUBO in cooperation with Coopers, and Lybrand. Alexandria, VA.

Sarason, S. B. (1972). <u>The creation of settings and future societies.</u> San Francisco: Jossey-Bass.

Schein, E. H. (1992). <u>Organization culture and leadership,</u> (2nd ed.). San Francisco: Jossey-Bass.

Schmidtlein, F. A. (1990). Why linking budgets to plans has proven difficult in higher education, <u>Planning, 18</u> (2), 89-90.

Schmidtlein, F. A. (1991, September). <u>Commonly accepted organization theories that mislead institutional researchers (and their client).</u> Paper delivered at the 13th International Forum, European Association for Institutional Research, Edinburgh, Scotland.

Sievers, B. (1994). <u>Work death and life itself.</u> Berlin: Walter de Gruyter.

Sjöstrand, S-E (1997). <u>The two faces of management.</u> Bungay, Suffolk, UK: International Thompson Business Press.

Smith, H. (1997, Nov.) <u>Topics of world religions.</u> A lecture at the Smithsonian Institution.

Smith, J. K. (1983, March). Quantitative versus qualitative research: An attempt to clarify the issue. <u>Educational Researcher, 10,</u> 6-13.

Spencer, C. (1977). <u>Blue collar.</u> Chicago: Lakeside Charter Books.

Taylor, F. W. (1923). <u>The principles of scientific management.</u> New York: Harper.

Thelin, J. R., & Yankovich, J. (1985). <u>Bricks and mortar: Architecture and the study of higher education.</u> Williamsburg, VA: The College of William and Mary.

Timberg, R. (1995). The nightingale's song. New York: Touchstone.

Vaill, P. B. (1989). Managing as a performing art. San Francisco: Jossey-Bass.

Van Manen, M. (1990). Researching lived experiences. Albany, NY: State University of New York Press.

Van Manen, M. (1992). Toward a discourse of heteronomy. Phenomenology + Pedagogy, 10, 252-255.

Versey, L. R., (1965). The emergence of the American university. Chicago: The University of Chicago Press.

von Clausewitz, C. (1984). On war. Princeton, NJ: Princeton University Press.

Wachterhauser, B. (1986). Hermeneutics and modern philosophy. Albany, NY: State University of New York.

Walker, D. E. (1979). The effective administrator. San Francisco: Jossey-Bass

Weick, K. E. (1991). Educational organizations as loosely coupled systems. In M. W. Peterson (Ed.), Organization and governance in higher education (4th ed., pp. 103-117). Needham Heights, MA: Ashe Reader Series, Ginn Press.
Whyte, D. (1994). The heart aroused. New York: Doubleday.

Winkler, A. M. (1992). The faculty workload question. Change, 24, (4), 36-34.

Winston, G. C. (1993). Why are capital costs ignored by colleges and universities and what are the prospects for change. In D. W. Breneman, L. L. Leslie, & R. E. Anderson (Eds.), <u>Finance in higher education</u> (pp. 217-226). Needham Heights, MA: Ashe Reader Series, Ginn Press.

Workman, L. (1992). The experience of policy. <u>Phenomenology + Pedagogy, 10,</u> 215-223.

www.ingramcontent.com/pod-product-compliance
Lightning Source LLC
Chambersburg PA
CBHW051508170526
45166CB00001B/437